NUCLEAR WAR FILMS

Edited by
Jack G. Shaheen

Foreword by Marshall Flaum

SOUTHERN ILLINOIS UNIVERSITY PRESS

Carbondale and Edwardsville

Feffer & Simons, Inc.
London and Amsterdam

Library of Congress Cataloging in Publication Data

Main entry under title:

Nuclear war films.

  Includes bibliographical references and index.
  1. War films—History and criticism. 2. Atomic warfare in motion pictures. I. Shaheen,
Jack G., 1935–
PN1995.9.W3N8   791.43'7   78-17984
ISBN 0-8093-0843-6
ISBN 0-8093-0879-7 pbk.

TO NAZARA AND MY CHILDREN

MICHAEL

AND

MICHELE

Contents

List of Illustrations

Foreword
By Marshall Flaum

Films are mirrors of our lives and times. During the course of this century, our changing society, our evolving attitudes and concerns— our history, in fact—have been reflected in our films. Perhaps less explicitly in features than in documentaries, but no less emphatically. Even the distortions and lies we often find in that celluloid mirror reveal some inescapable truths not only about those who created the falsity, but about those who demanded it and avidly paid for it at the box office. As such, the motion picture is fit study for the historian and the sociologist as much as it is for the film student.

In the broad study of the motion picture art and its relation to our collective history in this century, it is perhaps most valuable to examine the motion picture forms that have persisted over the years—the genre films. These are the films that fall into particular groups and categories, all within their category sharing similar motifs and similar styles. Since the endurance of these forms is determined by the degree of our response to them, they may be seen to significantly reveal our psychological, sociological, and political condition at any given point in our time.

In recent years there has been a proliferation of film books, although mostly of frivolous nature, with a heavy emphasis on nostalgia. There is nothing profoundly wrong with this, for when all is said and done, through the years movies indeed seem to have been our "best entertainment" and as a natural consequence, the films of the past do evoke the pleasant, bittersweet glow of nostalgia. Yet occasionally a serious analytical work like this appears that dares to probe beneath the surface of movie glamour and nostalgia to suddenly illuminate our existence in a meaningful exploration of an aspect of the cinematic art.

Much has been written about such film genres as the western, the science-fiction film, the gangster film, the screwball comedy, the horror film, and the like—but not until now has there been a critical study of the films dealing with nuclear war. This is a comparatively new genre, unhappily dictated by the way we live now in the latter part of the twentieth century. Let us hope that during our lifetime we may see these films also relegated from the area of current concern to the harmless realm of reflective nostalgia.

Preface

The analysis of the genre of nuclear motion pictures—features, documentaries, and educational short films—should enhance our ability to perceive, criticize, and appreciate the nuclear film in a disciplined and creative manner. This study is intended to be more than merely a collection of essays. No single composition speaks to all dimensions of the topic, but taken together, the collection presents a comprehensive view of the nuclear film image.

When one considers the far-reaching effects of atomic war on the lives of everyone, it is interesting to observe that Hollywood has produced relatively few films dealing with the subject. With most feature films there is a strong tendency to misrepresent historical fact and to dramatize romance, although each offers some nuclear awareness and did attract millions of theatergoers at a time when American attitudes were directed toward civil defense and the cold war.

Interestingly, the number of features concerned with the nuclear question decreased as the proliferation of nuclear weapons increased. From 1946 through 1965, feature films that exaggerated nuclear catastrophies appeared on theater screens, the majority being shown in the early 1960s. Abruptly after 1965, the genre films were no longer being released.

It was at this point that the television documentary began examining the nuclear dilemma. Most documentaries provided objective analyses of the arms race. Some producers offered historic gloss-over and exaggerated events. Others questioned the necessity of maintaining arms superiority. They, through biased editing, depicted military leaders and notable scientists favoring the expansion of nuclear defenses as being radical and irrational.

In addition to the feature and documentary are educational short films, which are personal statements made by individual artists working independently of the major studios and television networks. Unfortunately, there are few nuclear films of this nature. Produced between 1956 and 1970, most educational short films have not been telecast or shown in movie theaters. They have, however, received limited screenings in schools and colleges.

The book is divided into two categories: 1) features, 2) documentaries and educational short films. The feature film tended to exploit the general awareness of the bomb's dreaded power. Some films attempted a factual presentation while others concentrated on fantasy as the primary vehicle for enhancing the plot. Few films dealt with civil defense, peaceful uses of atomic energy, or radiation. Technology was the dominant factor; it was presented as inherently evil and would become more devastating if not controlled.

Two exceptional feature films avoiding the standard technology-as-evil theme are *Dr. Strangelove* and *Hiroshima, Mon Amour*. Both films possess a consistent and convincing narrative, penetrating human relationship insights, a fluid cinematic style, and an intellectual viewpoint. *Dr. Strangelove*, revealing the insanity of the nuclear arms race, presents a horrifyingly possible view of future holocausts, while *Hiroshima, Mon Amour* explores war and its effects on humanity.

The most commonly exploited theme is that of survival, as in *Five, The World, the Flesh, and the Devil, On the Beach,* and *Panic in Year Zero*. With the exception of Stanley Kramer's *On the Beach*, these films fail to heighten one's awareness of the nuclear problem.

Fail Safe, The Bedford Incident, and *The Day the Earth Caught Fire* focus on man's inability to control his technology; while *Ladybug, Ladybug* examines the behavior of children during a hypothetical nuclear attack. *The Beginning or the End*, a simple fictionalized treatment of atomic history, primarily illuminates romance. Thus, the nuclear feature film image, though mirroring American attitudes of the period in which they were produced, fluctuated between dreams and destruction.

The significance of the film image serves as an important social-political function. As Dorothy B. Jones wrote in 1945: "Traditionally, the motion picture industry has maintained that the primary function of the Hollywood film is to entertain. However, in a world shattered by conflict it has become increasingly evident that only through solidly founded and dynamic understanding among the peoples of the world can we establish and maintain an enduring peace. At the same time it has become clear that the film can play an important part in the creation of One World."[1]

Inherent in most nuclear feature films is one basic warning—man should not rely on technology at the expense of humanity and civilization. Ironically, despite an ever-growing arms race, by the middle 1960s nuclear destruction had lost its appeal as a theme for feature films.

America's initial documentary series to consider seriously the impact of nuclear warfare was *Air Power*. In November 1956, the first program chronicled the defensive action that might be taken in the event of an air attack. The show concluded with a shot of an A-bomb explosion. The film clip, however, began in the midst of the blast. The reason for excluding the initial frames was that an expert could analyze "an A-bomb's content and performance merely by seeing the first four frames of the explosion."[2] Such beliefs, because of the secrecy surrounding the bomb, were commonplace in the middle 1950s.

It was not until 1965 that a television documentary, Fred Freed's *The Decision to Drop the Bomb*, examined the moral military implications of atomic weaponry. Interpreting the documentary is similar to defining an ongoing form of art; useful in indicating its concerns and raising significant questions, but limiting and therefore not entirely convincing. Nevertheless the documentary is purposeful. Its emphasis is usually on factual content rather than on escapism. Television documentaries, such as Freed's *Decision*, advanced our awareness of the nuclear problem by focusing on historical, social, and scientific perceptions.

Not all documentaries were successful. Freed's next program, *Countdown to Zero* (1966), was concerned with the proliferation of nuclear weapons. Several months before he died he explained his approach to *Countdown*, why it failed, and the necessity of maintaining objective cinematic expression.

From 1969 to 1973, three additional network documentaries studied the problem in depth. The documentaries were *Footnotes on the Atomic Age, Arms and Security: How Much Is Enough?* and *And When the War Is Over—The American Military in the 70's*. Each program subtly

urged a restructuring of nuclear power and suggested the longer the
arms race continues, the less security we have. *Arms and Security*,
the ABC documentary, is now available for purchase only; the cost is
over five hundred dollars.

Five of six nonnetwork documentaries are not easily obtained for
educational screenings. National Educational Television's "NET Journal": *Hiroshima-Nagasaki*, for example, was aired only once by the
Public Broadcasting Service. The documentary may not now be shown
for any purpose, commercial or educational, and the prospects for
future screenings are remote.[3]

The British Broadcasting Corporation's two documentaries, *The War
Game* and *Rumours of War*, concentrate respectively on the study of
the consequences of a holocaust in Great Britain and on the humanistic
problems facing men who have daily access to nuclear arsenals. Although produced by the BBC specifically for television, *The War Game*
to date has not been televised. It has received educational and theatrical
distribution. *Rumours* may only be purchased from its distributor; the
fee is more than five hundred dollars.

Another BBC film, Robert J. Lifton's *To Die, To Live*, was broadcast in Great Britain in 1975 and is now available in the United States.
The documentary, based on Lifton's text, *Death in Life*, offers a detailed psychohistorical study of Hiroshima survivors. It is not available
for preview or rental, but for purchase only at eight hundred dollars
per print.

A Japanese documentary, *Hiroshima: A Document of the Atomic
Bombing*, is available for educational screenings and may be rented at
a nominal fee. But there is usually a six-months waiting period, as
the American distributor has only one film print. *Document*, an intense
portrayal of history, illustrates the human tragedy of Hiroshima.

One nonnetwork documentary is readily available—usually without a
rental fee. Produced by the Institute for American Strategy, *Only the
Strong* advocates an increase in military armaments. It was rejected by
the three major networks. However, *Strong* is being widely circulated
on college campuses and has received hundreds of telecasts by local
network affiliated stations and independents.

The educational short film is confronted with similar distribution
problems. Unlike the documentary, these films, lasting less than thirty
minutes, have been greatly ignored in cinema literature. "Creators of
short films are much like poets," notes David Sohn in *Film: The*

Creative Eye. "Their eyes are not on large commercial markets; they *have* to make their films, as a poet *has* to write a poem."[4]

The producers of educational short films have both disadvantages and advantages over feature and documentary film makers. A short nonfeature film is handicapped because it does not usually have the available audiences of the other two. Conversely, it does not have to extend dramatic situations to satisfy commercial time requirements. An educational film need not be structured to reach contrived climaxes, as is the case with televised documentaries and other films.[5]

The finest of short films are concise, primarily subjective films of experimentation, and involve experiences that stand the test of repeated viewing. They contain live action and animation. Sometimes they are wordless, the message or theme developed by visuals and music, as in Julian Biggs's *23 Skidoo*.

Biggs's filmic poem is discussed with *H-Bomb over U.S.*, *A Short Vision*, and *The Hole* in the "War in Short" essay. *H-Bomb over U.S.* and *A Short Vision* are fresh and creative, suggesting the effects of a hypothetical nuclear aftermath. In John and Faith Hubley's *The Hole*, a humorous animated film, the theme is vividly evident—mankind must disarm. Betty Jean Lifton's sensitive *A Thousand Cranes: Children of Hiroshima* is about young people in Japan who regularly distribute pamphlets and correspond with world leaders in an effort to encourage peace.

Unlike most short films, Erik Barnouw's *Hiroshima-Nagasaki— August, 1945* employs stock footage to convey the overpowering nuclear horror. Despite international acclaim, Barnouw's film was rejected by the major commercial networks. Hundreds of copies, however, have been sold to universities and schools at a nominal fee.

Still another view of the holocaust is presented in two films produced and distributed by the United States Army, *The Atom Strikes* and *A Tale of Two Cities*. No attempt is made to focus on humans; instead, the films examine the bomb's effects on the physical ruins of Hiroshima and Nagasaki.

The nuclear genre, embracing feature, documentary, and educational short films, possesses different sets of values and themes. Although each film illustrates a basic concern for the bomb, the artificiality of the film image tempers the harsh realities of nuclear destruction.

In previous critical literature on film there have been only occasional articles concerned with how motion pictures have portrayed nuclear war. This work, apparently, is the initial collection of critical essays concerned specifically with nuclear films. Teachers, journalists, and film makers, representing diverse backgrounds, interests, and points of view, have contributed.

The text may be used in a variety of educational situations: as an overview for educators in selected disciplines; as a reference work; for college courses and film festivals, high school classrooms, military departments of service academies, ROTC programs, peace studies seminars, special student-teacher workshops; and as a resource for research or by those interested in film.

Beyond the significance of teaching, the films reflect an important era of film history. Screened as part of a collective study, with discussions afterward, the films themselves may become a means of instruction. Films receiving detailed discussion are readily available in 16-mm prints for rental and viewing. A list of the films, their distributors, and film credits may be found in "Distributors and Credits."

The investigation does not contain analyses of all nuclear genre films, notably Japanese features. I have attempted to encompass the more significant films produced since 1946. Other films not discussed are those possessing both an abundance of science and an abundance of fiction. Such fantasy films contained illogical visions: hooded, deformed villains, giant insects, and other monsters.

During the final quarter of the twentieth century, the nuclear genre appears diminished in scope and importance. The book is designed to encourage a reasoned and thoughtful understanding of nuclear films, to convey not only the diversity of genre themes but a sense of the fragility of human life.

My deepest gratitude to Professors Robert W. Duncan and William J. Tudor, who provided continued guidance. Also, I wish to thank Bea Drummond, James Hall, Jill Leitner, Melissa McCanna, Mark Morgan, Dick Richmond, and Jody Stone for their assistance. I am especially grateful to my wife, Bernice, whose understanding and love was a constant source of encouragement.

JACK G. SHAHEEN

Edwardsville, Illinois
January 1978

Notes on Contributors

PHILIP BANDY has taught communications at Lake Michigan College and is now director of Audience Development for WOTV, Grand Rapids, Michigan.

DONALD BITTNER is a professor of history at the Command and Staff College, Quantico, Virginia.

ROBERT W. DUNCAN is a professor of English, Southern Illinois University, Edwardsville.

RAMEY ELLIOT is a professional, independent film maker.

JAMES HALL is a graduate of the Mass Communications Department at Southern Illinois University, Edwardsville.

MARK HALL, author of *Broadcast Journalism*, teaches courses in film appreciation and documentary film at Butte College, Durham, California. He recently completed a manuscript that examines the impact of media systems on personal life-styles.

JOSEPH KEYERLEBER, formerly a motion picture director for Associated Filmmakers International, currently produces special programs for the Justice Department.

GEORGE W. LINDEN, professor of philosophy at Southern Illinois University, Edwardsville, is a film critic, poet, and the author of *Reflections on the Screen*.

ERNEST F. MARTIN is an associate professor of journalism at the University of Kansas.

GEORGE A. MASTROIANNI, coauthor of *Issues in Broadcasting*, is an associate professor of mass communications, California State College, Fullerton.

WILLIAM MEYER, formerly an English instructor at Southern Illinois University, Edwardsville, currently teaches at Parks College, Cahokia, Illinois.

MARK W. NELSON has worked as a radio news director and is now a teacher of communications at Collinsville, Illinois.

FRANK W. OGLESBEE is an associate professor of mass communications at Loyola University in New Orleans.

H. WAYNE SCHUTH is an associate professor of mass communications, University of New Orleans.

JACK G. SHAHEEN is professor of mass communications, Southern Illinois University, Edwardsville.

JODY STONE, in addition to reviewing films, worked as a newspaper reporter and is currently an associate editor for *Framing and Fine Art*.

RICHARD TAYLOR, a film maker at Southern Illinois University, Edwardsville, also writes cinema criticism.

EUGENE M. URAM, a documentary film producer, has taught cinema at the University of Wisconsin and Lindenwood College, St. Charles, Missouri.

KAMIL WINTER, formerly director of news and national affairs for Czechoslovakia's National Television Network, is an associate professor of mass communications, Southern Illinois University, Edwardsville.

MICHAEL G. WOLLSCHEIDT is a producer-director of documentaries and newscasts with KTVH-TV, Wichita, Kansas.

DAVID G. YELLIN, author of *Special: Fred Freed and the Television Documentary*, is a professor of Broadcasting and Film at Memphis State University.

1

FEATURE FILMS

1

JACK G. SHAHEEN AND RICHARD TAYLOR

The Beginning or the End

The first American motion picture concerning nuclear war was Metro-Goldwyn-Mayer's *The Beginning or the End*. The film proposed to educate and inform the citizenry about the development of the new atomic age. Presented in a pseudodocumentary style (a fake "News of the Day" feature is employed, in addition to authentic newsreel footage of the 1940s), *Beginning* received criticism from numerous cinema reviewers. Perhaps its subject, the development of the atomic bomb, merited additional analysis before filming; it was produced in 1946, only one year after the atomic explosions over Hiroshima and Nagasaki.

Interestingly, Paramount Studios also sought to film the story of the bomb's development, but MGM was given the opportunity to treat this important subject.[1] Most of the film focuses on the monologues of scientists, politicians and military men. A traditional love-interest story is also added; a young scientist (Tom Drake) constantly questions the morality of the bomb, while explaining to his bride why he is unable to spend more time at home. As explicated in *Life*, the "young scientist indicates to his unhappy wife that he'd be home for dinner more often if it weren't so darned hard to figure out this chain-reaction stuff."[2] As is so often the case in both factual and fiction feature films of the forties and fifties, a romantic interlude was mandatory.

Promoted by MGM's publicity department as "the story of the most HUSH-HUSH secret of all time," and as the true story of the A-bomb, *Beginning* fails to offer an honest, documented version of history.[3] In the opening sequence, viewers are informed that *Beginning* has been produced specifically for the purpose of being placed in a time capsule, which is not to be opened for five hundred years. From this unusual beginning, the film proceeds to guide one through the entire development of the A-bomb: Nobel Prize physicist Enrico Fermi's Chicago experiment; President Franklin D. Roosevelt's decision to begin the Manhattan Project; the collaboration of science and industry in constructing the bomb; the initial test at Alamogordo, New Mexico; the destruction of Hiroshima and the morality of the decision.

The essential rudiments of atomic fission are offered, followed by the history of atomic research, nuclear energy's potential to assist the world, and the moral obligations of those scientists harnessing the atom's energy. However, to give the film authenticity, payments were made to prominent nuclear physicists and other dignitaries for permission to impersonate them with actors in the film. Hume Cronyn portrayed Dr. J. Robert Oppenheimer; a lesser-known actor, Ludwig Stossel, played Albert Einstein; and Godfrey Teare was selected to play Franklin D. Roosevelt. Brian Donlevy was cast as Gen. Leslie R. Groves, while two actors, Roman Bohnen and Art Baker, were employed to play President Harry S Truman.[4]

Agnes Moorhead was cast as a scientist working on the bomb. But legal problems with the actual scientist she was portraying prompted MGM to cut her scenes from the film.[5] Publicity stills of Miss Moorhead as the scientist, however, were made with the hope that the legalities could be solved.

This attempt at historical re-creation, best seen in Edward R. Murrow's television series, "You Are There," was not successfully transformed onto the movie screen. Conversely, a 1946 *March of Time* episode, *Atomic Power*, succeeds in dramatizing the development of atomic weapons. The reason for its success was that those scientists, government and military officials who were involved with the project appeared instead of actors. It was one thing to hear and see a prominent scientist or president, but quite another to view actors as impersonators. Thus, the authority of the statements and events in *Beginning* tend to lose credibility.

President Roosevelt, for example, is treated as an idol; his scenes are directed in a highly exaggerated manner (perhaps this approach, by director Norman Taurog, was used because Eleanor Roosevelt believed that no one could adequately portray her late husband on the screen.)[6]

Unfortunately the impact of these segments is reduced. This weakness is apparent in the scene of the president rushing to call British

The Beginning or the End. Courtesy of The Museum of Modern Art/Film Stills Archive

Prime Minister Winston Churchill to share with him the good news that the bomb is possible. In yet another sequence, the president suggests sending a memo with information on the Manhattan Project to Vice-President Truman, but he delays the writing and exits to pose for his portrait. Director Taurog then cuts to Roosevelt's dog, who sadly whines. (Earlier, the spaniel whined disapprovingly on hearing the probable cost of the Manhattan Project—two billion dollars.) Those knowing and appreciating the essence of the project and the conflict experienced by Roosevelt are not prepared for such sophomoric direction or cutaways that distract from the significance of important decisions.

The film also fails to adequately document the bomb's initial development. The first run of the atomic pile (at Stagg Field in Chicago) was probably the most exciting scientific experiment in history. The film's scientists are dutifully catalogued (with a few additions), principally Enrico Fermi and Arthur H. Compton, Chicago's director of the Metallurgical Atomic Project. There the resemblance ends.[7] The experiments reflect a preface to fictional drama. The film gives the impression of a congenial family reunion; but the actual event, according to eyewitnesses, was unbearably tense, heightened by the clicking of neutron counters and Fermi's careful instructions to his assistants. The film's reenactment offers instead loud, buzzing sounds, presumably caused by the splitting of uranium atoms. The laboratory setting resembles a mysterious room designed to develop science fiction melodrama. The effect is unsatisfying and the awesome importance of the moment is lost.

The visuals of the atomic pile are falsely depicted. One sees an impressive stack of lead shielding and control rods; the actual pile was covered with balloon cloth.[8] Even the bomb is misrepresented; it is shown as a sleek gleaming object. (On the day of the first H-bomb explosion in 1954 a newspaper advertisement read, "The bomb's brilliant gleam reminds me of the brilliant gleam Beacon Wax gives to floors. It's a science marvel.")[9] As with the advertisement, the streamlined, chrome-plated special bomb is merely an illusion of *Beginning*'s special effects department, bearing no resemblance to the actual weapon.

Despite the film's numerous distortions and failings, there are some highly credible moments. Cinematically, the initial blasts at Alamogordo and the Hiroshima explosion, as created by A. Arnold Gillespie, are visually stunning.

Gillespie's effects captured the essence of the atomic weapon's eerie splendor. Witnessing an atomic bomb explosion in the Nevada desert, an American soldier wrote: "A magnificent cloud arose from the desert floor . . . and spiraled toward the sun. It was work beyond man. No artist ever held its palette of colors. No magician could have mastered its surprises. It was a divinity. Or the Devil. . . . We were, for one afternoon, men who had stared full into Fear. We saw Annihilation. We foresaw Doomsday."[10]

Gillespie, who received an Oscar for his effects, "created in miniature an A-bomb blast so realistic it fooled the Manhattan Project people and was later used by the U.S. Air Force in a training film." Interestingly, all the technical details were classified at the time; Gillespie simply placed "his camera underwater, inside a tank, and shot his holocaust with exploding sacks of dye."[11]

Sagacious editing also helps create authentic moments of realism; the actors' reactions are believable, while the restrained use of music enhances the compelling effectiveness of the mushroom cloud.

MGM deserves some credit for creating the film. There were numerous political and "security" considerations that had to be discussed. By 1946, not all of the information concerning the Manhattan Project had been declassified.[12] Some politicians contended they had the right to comment on the film because of its political implications. Military leaders voiced concern over certain scenes because the atomic bomb remained a high-priority risk. Thus, in order to please everyone, *Beginning* opted for a consensus on matters of historical significance.

Several members of the military, for example, were not pleased with the scene in which President Truman is told the atomic bomb is ready. They argued that it appeared Truman gave no consideration to the problem; that on hearing the bomb could be employed, he immediately ordered its use against Japan. President Truman's advisors also requested that certain scenes be reshot. They believed that actor Roman Bohnen portrayed Truman with too much military bearing. It was decided actor Art Baker should replace Bohnen. To create a more sensitive figure, Baker was given additional dialogue by writer Frank Wead; one additional line referred to "many sleepless nights in the White House worrying about dropping the bomb." Also, the reshot scenes show only the back of Truman's head.[13]

In the prerelease print of *Beginning*, a crew member asks Colonel Nixon (Robert Walker): "Is it true that if you fool around with this stuff

(atomic equipment) long enough, you don't like girls anymore?"
Walker responded: "I hadn't noticed it."[14] Fortunately, this sequence
was omitted. In another instance, censorship is used to sell tickets. To
promote the pseudo secrecy of the atomic project and the military's
concern, a publicity still depicts a scaffolding holding the bomb for its
initial test. The bomb, however, is covered by a gigantic "Censored"
sign. The poster suggests that the very sight of the bomb will reveal
secrets of the atom to the moviegoer.[15] Thus, viewers are able to "see
the bomb" only after purchasing tickets.

Beginning contends that the men who developed the world's most
awesome weapon were ordinary dedicated human beings. The young
experimenter, Matt, is featured as the only scientist who questions the
use of the weapon. Yet, confident his colleagues and superiors have
a firmer grasp of the situation, he willingly leaves his wife to work near
an airstrip from which the bomber *Enola Gay* will depart. While arming
the bomb, Matt accidentally contracts a lethal dose of radiation. At
the last moment, however, he successfully reaches inside the bomb to
prevent a premature detonation. He soon dies, but not before giving a
friend the customary "final letter." His last words are, "That's what I
get for building this thing." In reality, the atomic bomb's first peacetime fatalities did occur in Los Alamos (Harry Daghlian, August 1945,
and Dr. Louis Slotin, June 1946; Daghlian's hands were swollen un-
believably, and the skin fell from his body in patches—doctors took
photographs for clinical use).[16]

Was writer Wead depicting Matt as martyr, one life sacrificed as the
price paid for the thousands killed in the atomic blast? Or was his death
merely contrived to create the situation wherein a posthumous letter
justifying further atomic experiments might be presented? The film fails
to answer these questions. Instead, it relies on sustaining the theme of
an earlier conversation between Matt and Colonel Nixon.

> MATT: "Most scientists don't really want to make the bomb."
> COLONEL: "Get it done before the Germans and Japs, then worry about
> the bomb."

The basic purpose of *The Beginning or the End* was to inform future
generations about the development of atomic energy, particularly as it
applies to warfare. Yet the film neglects to discuss the real problems of
the atomic potential and fails to examine the matter of control—military, civilian, or international.

Instead, the viewer's sympathy is directed to Matt, the fictional young scientist who died while working on the bomb. The film's final scene takes place before the Lincoln Memorial. Here, Matt's widow (Beverly Tyler) reads the posthumous letter. We hear Matt's voice, his face is superimposed in the background. Matt shares his hope that atomic energy will be used for the betterment of mankind—he no longer doubts the role of atomic energy. Uncertain of the morality of military nuclear development, Matt willingly supports it because his superiors know what they are doing.

In an era that pleads for rational thinking, *Beginning* offers instead moments of excessive sentimentality. The result is a stock cliché ending for a stock cliché motion picture. An accurate presentation of nuclear physics, much less the A-bomb, is not presented. The bomb served as good publicity and an unusual background for a love story. Conversely, Stephen Peet's 1976 BBC documentary, *The Day the Sun Blowed Up*, examines the first test of the atomic bomb through the recollections of those who worked on the project and those who lived in the area where the test was conducted. Various anecdotes provide perspective; the scientists are humanized—Fermi played volleyball while Oppenheimer and General Groves washed their own dishes. Little-known facts about the bomb are revealed: in Los Alamos, everyone called it "the gadget." Initially, the gadget was to explode inside a two-hundred ton steel bottle called "Jumbo." One of the film's scientists expressed doubts about the gadget's performance, stating: "We were not exactly sure if it would work." Oppenheimer was also doubtful, placing a ten-dollar bet that the gadget would fail. Interestingly, it wasn't until weeks after the successful test that many of the scientists first began to think about the morality of the bomb.

Several scenes in *Beginning* even falsify history; Matt, for example, is shown convincing Albert Einstein that he should write the president: Einstein's letter is supposedly the sole reason for the Manhattan Project.[17] In another sequence, the *Enola Gay* is seen encountering heavy flak resistance over Hiroshima. Historical records contain no reference to such resistance.

A later MGM film, *Above and Beyond*, also contained historical inaccuracies. The film unsuccessfully examined the physical and mental struggles of the *Enola Gay*'s pilot, Col. Paul Tibbetts (Robert Taylor). As with *Beginning*, the result was a conglomeration of romantics and melodrama; the moral aspects of Hiroshima were neglected.

Beginning failed to include other significant issues. On July 21, sixty atomic scientists signed a petition urging that the bomb should not be used against Japan without a convincing warning and an opportunity to surrender.[18] In the film, no mention is made of any scientist, with the exception of Matt, objecting to the use of the bomb.

Also, using fake newsreels with authentic news scenes only serves to distract from the film's worthwhile intentions. Some of the dialogue is shallow and without purpose. Colonel Nixon, for example, asks Matt what would happen if the safety rods on the atomic pile should fail: "We might lose something," he responds. "What?" says Nixon. "Chicago," concludes the scientist.[19]

"The picture will do no great harm unless it discourages the making of better pictures on the same subject,"[20] noted *Time*. Yet inaccurate documentation and an abundance of romantic sentiment deprived the movie of the authoritative quality claimed by its producers. Failing as both a document of history and entertainment, *The Beginning or the End* seldom achieves its noble intentions.

2

ERNEST F. MARTIN

Five

The first film maker to produce a movie about survivors of a nuclear World War III was Arch Oboler, one of radio's innovative and prolific authors who joined the pilgrimage to Hollywood in the 1940s.[1] In 1951, Oboler wrote, directed, and produced *Five*, a futuristic vision of the world "after the bomb." *Five* is based on Oboler's two-character radio drama, "The Word," which has a similar theme.

The importance of *Five* to the nuclear war genre is not in the cinematic virtuosity of the director, not the contrived plot, not the allegory on racial tensions. The importance is the influence of *Five* in the development of the cinematic attitude toward atomic war. For better or for worse, *Five* is another reminder of the filmic message sold to audiences about nuclear war.

Five is a melodrama with unusual potential. Following a nuclear holocaust, a global cloak of radioactive fallout annihilates all human life except five fortunates—or unfortunates—who are left to inherit what is left of the earth. Fortuitously, all five gather at a mountaintop lodge on the California coast. The survivors are a microcosm of society: an idealistic young Dartmouth graduate (William Phipps); a hysterical pregnant girl (Susan Douglas); a gentle black bank attendant (Charles Lampkin); an elderly cashier typifying the white-collar worker (Earl Lee); and an arrogant sportsman-fascist explorer (James Anderson). The gathering of the group in one rustic location tends to stagger, rather than excite, the imagination.

Oboler concentrates on the world's moral and physical conflicts after the new beginning. The elderly cashier dies soon after the film begins. Charles, the sole black in the group, is murdered by Eric later, deftly disposing of the race problem inherent in the plot. Eric, the sportsman-fascist, then succumbs to radioactive poisoning. Thus, the young man and woman are left to give the world a second chance.

Five illustrates several characteristics of Hollywood's attitude toward atomic war. First, the film offers a pessimistic mood about the future of the world in an atomic age. A newspaper headline in the movie explains that the world powers collapse under the strain of the nuclear threat. With collapse, the final destructive munitions are brought into focus. As the opening credits instruct, "The deadly wind passeth over it and it is gone . . . and the place thereof shall know it no more." The pessimistic mood is also demonstrated when young, idealistic Michael says, "We're in a dead world . . . and I'm glad it's dead . . . Cheap honky-tonk of a world." Also, the direction of morality and politics of the contemporary world community is intensified by the assumption that there will be total—or near-total—human destruction "when the buttons are pushed." The idea that everyone would die in a nuclear war appears to be an overstatement, creating misconceptions about potential nuclear warfare.

This pessimism is a type of fatalism. In *Five*, Oboler examines a world in which technology and humanism did not (and perhaps could not) peacefully coexist. However, fatalism appears unavoidable in most nuclear war films—without it there could be no story. For a story to exist at all, the earth must be nearly destroyed or likely to be demolished by the stupidity of its own inhabitants. Yet atomic destruction is only a part of the quandary brought about by atomic power. Few films that followed *Five* were concerned with the peaceful uses of the atom and radiation hazards that could result.[2] A single concept was usually employed—the end of the world brought about by technical knowledge divorced from humanitarianism. *Five* typified the nuclear war film, presenting pessimistic visions of overwhelming proportions for the future.

The most moving and effective scene in *Five* occurred when Eric and Roseanne were moving through a dead city, past busses, cars littered with skeletons, in a macabre search for the girl's husband. Here the film achieves some visual impact. Empathy and realism are effectively conveyed by focusing on individuals in desperate search of a never-to-be-found reality.

While occasionally emotionally gripping, *Five* fails to treat the prospect of atomic war by not being concerned with the militarism that caused the initial nuclear attack. It does not question the inevitability

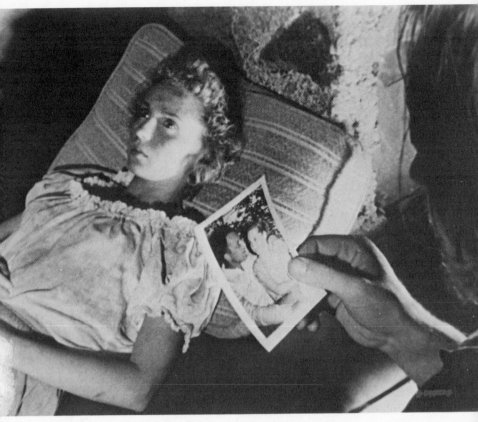

Five. Courtesy of The Museum of Modern Art/Film Stills Archive

of war nor the concentrated arms race. Instead, *Five* attempts to depict an outrageously absurd reality of a nuclear aftermath in a romantic, emotional manner, suggesting mankind will continue—no matter what.

Perhaps any film with a theme concerning the aftermath of nuclear war is inherently a plea for understanding and peace. The argument might be valid if the theme required a realistic look at the aftermath. James Baldwin contends "movies are designed not to trouble but to reassure; they do not reflect reality. . . . They . . . weaken our ability to deal with the world as it is, ourselves as we are."[3]

The reality of war should shock viewers. The result of deathly struggles should not be passed off by *Five*'s prologue: "The deadly wind passeth over it and it is gone . . . and the place thereof shall know it no more." The reality of nuclear war should not conclude with an epilogue from Revelation 21: "And I saw a new heaven and a new earth . . . and there shall be no more death, no more sorrow . . . No more tears . . . Behold! I make all things new!" The passages suggest we should not be troubled, mankind will survive.

The difficulty in ascertaining responsible attitudes toward atomic war is partially attributable to the fact that film, after all, dramatizes events. In *Five*, several distortions are evident. One of the most blatant is the liberty taken with physical probabilities after a nuclear blast. In the film, all vegetable and mineral matter survives, yet human beings disintegrate immediately into skeletons. The pregnant Roseanne, for example, would not have been protected by staying behind a lead shield for hours. The radiation would either kill or mutate the fetus. Oboler overlooked the realities for the emotional potential the baby offered. There are similar distortions in Jim McBride's *Glen and Randa* (1971). Unlike *Five*, the film begins a half century after the blast, yet fails to explain how or why the young couple, Glen and Randa, (Randa, like Roseanne, is pregnant), are still alive. They roam the country, encountering sundry items of a broken civilization. Director McBride, like Oboler, offers, without justification, physical improbabilities: Camel cigarettes, dry matches, a broken television set, and comic book, all intact fifty years later. McBride's vision of the postatomic world is similar to Oboler's; both men are concerned with man's ability to impose his own order on the universe.[4]

Five, however, emphasizes the necessity of social relationships by showing the destruction of the contemporary world as reflected in human behavior. The film could be viewed as a comment on racial tensions rather than a comment about the effects of atomic catastrophe. The racial conflict is generally static, and serves little interest. The explorer, Eric, for example, was on Mount Everest when the fateful bomb exploded. He supposedly traveled halfway around the world to find a small pocket of mankind. On discovering that one part of that group of mankind is black, a conflict immediately develops. It subsides only when Eric momentarily acknowledges that mankind should not repeat its mistakes. The change in heart is short-lived, however. Eric deliberately kills Charles.

Ranald MacDougall's 1959 film, *The World, the Flesh, and the Devil*, also stresses the racial question in a nuclear aftermath. The heavy reliance on typical social relationships raises the question: why concentrate on those characters surviving nuclear catastrophies relatively unscathed? The emphasis seems misplaced. There is nothing to be learned from observing the performers in their fearfully unique situation.

Five typifies the romanticized version of the effects of nuclear war. As Robert Hatch wrote: "What we fear from the next war is famine and disease and bestiality; tyranny and the loss of whatever human dignity we have inherited from past generations. To suppose that the atom will bring quick death for the millions and a bright, clean world for a bright, clean boy and girl to repopulate is to tell a fairy story to the soft-minded."[5]

It is a fatally flawed film—flawed by typical dream-spinning. The only real function of Oboler's nuclear catastrophe appears to be an arrangement for the hero to get the heroine to fall into his arms. Everyone else is killed off in one melodramatic way or another. Even the baby is eliminated—clearing the way for a romantic ending. A new Adam and Eve are hurled back from a technological age to work the soil. In a typical pseudoromantic fashion, they face the future with love in their hearts and determination etched on their faces.

Ultimately, the romanticized plot floundered as it reached its conclusion. *Five* was the first of the nuclear war genre to have this problem, but it was not the last. (In *The World, the Flesh, and the Devil*, a similar romanticized ending was used.) The representation that "life will go on" ultimately imparts an air of falseness, of unreality to such endings. *Five* never suggests that nuclear war would be a disaster.

Perhaps we require too much by demanding that fiction movies do what they cannot. Yet, must such films contain strenuous, romantic plots, be "larger than life," and take poetic license with technical facts? Colin Young, analyzing the role of war films, said: "Perhaps we should agree that Hollywood should be left to its own devices, and we should search for other patterns, other approaches to production and to the audience, than through the Hollywood fiction drama."[6]

Although the United States genre of nuclear war films began in 1946 with Norman Taurog's *The Beginning or the End*, Arch Oboler's *Five* (1951) should be remembered as the initial nuclear war film to illustrate a futuristic vision of a society and its inhabitants in the aftermath of a nuclear holocaust. Other films would unsuccessfully emulate Oboler's theme, using atomic destruction and the threat of destruction to maintain interest. Despite its weaknesses, Oboler's concern with his five selected people, their aspirations and hopes for a renewed civilization, is commendable. Although he employed an abundance of gloss and romance, he most probably did so hoping that *Five* might create a new awareness. He wished to convey a concern for the possible destruction of his civilization by atomic bombs.

3

H. WAYNE SCHUTH

Hiroshima, Mon Amour

To be intellectually or philosophically interesting, the theme of a film should shed new light on the familiar, or present a truly new idea. A film based exclusively on the premise that war is bad usually fails as a valid and lasting work of art. *Hiroshima, Mon Amour* tells us something new about *why* war is destructive to both victor and vanquished and can thus claim a lasting place in cinematic art.[1]

Alain Resnais's film is about rebirth—the rebirth of a city and the rebirth of a woman. Both have suffered tragedies and both are reborn. Hiroshima, the symbol of the atom bomb blast, of death, is played off against Mon Amour, my love, the symbol of hope and life.

The story, set in the present, focuses on a French actress who comes to Hiroshima to make a film about peace. She meets a Japanese architect with whom she has a brief affair. During the affair, the architect reminds her of a love from her past, when she was young in her hometown, Nevers, during World War II. Her love was a German soldier who was later killed. The woman was ridiculed because of her affair with an enemy of France (her hair cut off, she was paraded through the streets); as a result, she suffered a temporary mental breakdown. The architect draws the story from her. She has been living with her memory of past tragic love, and as she confides in the architect, she is able to put the former experience in perspective, free herself from the past, and become a new woman.

It is not by chance that Resnais's hero is an architect who helps to build Hiroshima as well as the woman's new consciousness, or that his heroine is an actress who plays roles in her real life until the affair with the architect. It is meaningful to the story as every detail is meaningful in this film. As Hiroshima is rebuilt, the girl is cured.

The film is also about forgetting; the conflict between the necessity of forgetting in order to live, and the importance of remembering in order to avoid the mistakes of the past. Resnais's film is one of the most moving statements on the human condition yet achieved in the contemporary cinema. As in his other films, Resnais plays the poet-philosopher, evoking a variety of moods, dealing with states of mind, and discussing important moral and social issues.[2]

During the film's first sequence, the man and woman are making love. Their arms are intertwined, and they are perspiring; it appears they are covered with ashes or fallout, thus equated with the tragedy of Hiroshima. She says to him that she saw the Atomic Museum, the hospital, the newsreels. He says to her that she knows nothing of Hiroshima. There are cuts to show us what she is talking about. This also helps the viewer to "get into her mind," to identify with her by knowing her thoughts, seeing what she has seen. She mentions she learned at the museum that on the second day after the bombing certain animal species crawled out from under the ashes. "On the fifteenth day, Hiroshima was carpeted with flowers, which sprang from the ashes with a vitality never before seen in flowers." The credits of the film are superimposed over a shot of plants growing from the sand (shown in negative image). The same shot (in a positive image) is shown during the woman's talk of Hiroshima. Resnais is saying to us that despite this tragedy, life can emerge with new vitality. The flowers are reborn.

She says, "Just as in love there is the illusion that it can never be forgotten. Like you, I have struggled with all my might against forgetting. Like you, I have forgotten." He replies, "You know nothing of Hiroshima," or "You can't understand my feelings since I was there." But, she has experienced a tragedy of her own, and although a personal tragedy, the same feelings of sadness and loss can be shared.

The past is ever impinging on the present. The woman sees things in the present that remind her of the past. The shape of the man's arm as he sleeps recalls the arm of her former lover in the same position. The shape of buildings in Hiroshima recalls the shape of buildings in Nevers.

Resnais made *Hiroshima, Mon Amour* on the tide of the French New Wave. This movement included François Truffaut, Jean Luc Godard,

Hiroshima, Mon Amour. Courtesy of Contemporary Films/McGraw-Hill

Jacques Demy, and Louis Malle. But Resnais stands apart from these other film makers in terms of his unique use of cinematic technique.

A major contribution to the contemporary cinema is the remarkable editing, infusing the past and the present. Instead of repeatedly using dissolves to indicate changes in time, Resnais cuts directly from present to past and back again. By suddenly introducing new episodes and repeating those episodes already seen in the film, Resnais breaks up the given time sequence. He thereby suggests the characters' thoughts and memories.[3] This not only carries the story but gives the viewer a feeling that the past and the present are combined, infused as one, which is exactly Resnais's point in regard to the man, the woman, and Hiroshima. His cuts are often triggered by similar compositions (the arm in the present, the arm in the past); moreover, he often ignores conventional cutting in the present to punctuate his statements. As Lee Bobker notes: "Resnais pieces fragments of past episodes into a fantastic jigsaw puzzle. The past thrusting itself into the present is the very substance of his cutting. The film communicates this to us because of the perfect use of the overlapping dialogue, the steady extension of the flashback scenes and the precise moment that the music is heard, providing clues and place."[4]

A major sequence in the film, which illustrates Resnais's unique editing technique, is found in one scene in which the man and woman are lying together. She inquires why he wants to know about her past. With regard to Nevers, he says: "It was there, I feel, you were so young, so very young, that you belonged to no one in particular, which I like. It was there, I feel, I almost lost you, and ran the risk of never knowing you at all. It was there, I feel, you started being the woman you still are today." During these sentences, which begin with the same words, "It was there, I feel," Resnais employs close-ups of the man in different positions. This violates a tradition of pictorial continuity, but in this scene it works. The music is low key, the words like poetry, the jump cuts punctuate the thoughts and are effective.

Resnais's cutting is also excellent when he shows the woman in Nevers as a girl, riding a bicycle. Her bicycle-riding remains constant, yet the locations change. Seven similar cuts appear in succession to show her, at various times, riding to meet her lover.

The film is well designed. Every element is there for a reason. For example, the man and woman are standing in a crowd watching the filming of a peace parade. It is important to keep in mind that a dead lover from the past is constantly influencing the woman's reactions to the present. The man tells the woman he thinks he loves her. In the frame, we see the man touching the woman, but also, next to the woman, another man, who is covered with black ashes; he is playing a victim of the bombing. The way Resnais composes the shot, however, the man in black looks like a shadow and reminds the viewer of the presence of the woman's former lover.

Another design element is Resnais's use of the visual motif. A visual motif is a visual symbol that recurs throughout the film to give it unity, and has significance to the film's theme. In *Hiroshima, Mon Amour*, the visual motif is a building with a shattered dome (a kind of memorial) that has been standing since the bombing. Resnais includes the building in many shots of the film and even has a model of it carried in the peace parade. It symbolizes the remnants of the old Hiroshima and, in particular, the outward shell of the woman. She has survived her tragedy. The shattered dome is also reminiscent of the hair shorn from the woman's head in Nevers. As the film progresses, the dome is seen less and less, being finally replaced by the new and modern buildings of Hiroshima.

In viewing *Hiroshima, Mon Amour*, one should be aware of what Resnais is doing with his audience and his characters. They forget the horrors of the past and go on to lead new lives. The initial shots of Hiroshima are quite brutal—newsreel footage of the destruction and victims. But as the film progresses, the viewer becomes involved in the personal story of the woman and also begins to forget the horror depicted in the beginning shots. Resnais's editing is of some assistance. The first part of the film contains many brief shots. Conversely, the final scenes contain many lengthy shots, which require additional concentration as the mood changes.

The following analyses of scenes reflect the brilliance of Resnais's meticulous design. At the beginning of the film, there are images of destruction, photographed at the Hiroshima Atomic Museum. Resnais shot a bicycle, twisted out of shape by the blast. He photographed human hair falling from the heads of victims. Both images relate to the Nevers story.

Here, where the lovers are intercut between visualizations of the woman's thoughts, tension is evoked within the viewer. The words, at times, resemble poetry; the music is at times hauntingly beautiful; while the visuals consist of the horrors of Hiroshima. The dissonance is intentional. A long tracking shot follows, through the new Hiroshima.

This shot is planned to give relief from the horrors just seen. She says to her lover, "You destroy me, you are good for me." The words mean precisely what they say. As her love increases, the original woman is destroyed, as a new woman is born. Thus, "You destroy me, you are good for me." Later, she says, "I feel the art of seeing has to be learned." And her lover teaches her to see.

She tells him that affairs, like the one she is having, happen to her— not very often—but they do happen. "I am fond of men," she says. He accepts this. She tells him about Nevers, how she was young, but also slightly mad. Out on the square in front of the hotel (appropriately named Hotel New Hiroshima), he asks to see her again. "The thought of not seeing you again . . . ever," he says. The same words are spoken later by the woman as she remembers her German lover.

He finds her again, working on the set of the peace film. She agrees to be with him one more time. As she watches the parade, she sees little girls marching along carrying paper doves. This reminds her of her own youth, and she cries. The man and woman are jostled by the crowd—a visual statement on their present state of mind.

At the man's home, they talk of their marriages. Both state they are happily married, but he says, "It is never that simple." The fact that marriage and her children are mentioned just once in the film, that the lines are thrown away (both are very sad when they say them), and that her present husband knows nothing of the Nevers story leads one to think that she plays a role in her marriage as she plays in the peace film. As they talk, the phone rings; they ignore it and make love.

She confides her former lover was German, not French. Notice how Resnais has set up the present lover and the past lover as former enemies of France: one Japanese, the other German. This makes the story more believable as she equates the Japanese man with the German. In a café, he asks, "Am I dead when you are in the cellar?" Here, clearly, her lover is equating himself with the German, and it works. She thinks of the two interchangeably until after the slapping scene. As the woman tells her story, we hear the sounds of Hiroshima and the café over the visuals of Nevers. As she becomes engrossed, the sounds of Hiroshima cease. The man slaps her to bring her out of her hysteria and back to reality; once again, the sounds of Hiroshima are heard over the subsequent shots of Nevers.

After she has finished telling him of Nevers and of her past, the man says, "One day when I have forgotten you, when other stories like this

happen again, as they are bound to, I'll think of you as the symbol of
love without memory. I'll remember this story as the anguish of forgetting. I already know it." This is important to Resnais's concept of
forgetting, for as one forgets, the stories and remembrances turn into
emotions, *love* without memory, the *anguish* of forgetting. Later in the
film, she confides, "As it was with him, I shall forget your eyes. Then,
as it was with him, your voice will go. Then, as it was with him, I shall
forget all of you. Bit by bit you will turn into a song." So she, too, will
experience the process of forgetting until it becomes like an emotion,
a song.

As they go onto the terrace of the café, one of the more touching
scenes in the film occurs. She says, "We'll probably die without meet-
ing again." He answers, "Probably, unless there is a war." She looks
in the mirror and says, "Fifteen years I've searched for an impossible
love since Nevers. See, I've forgotten you." She leaves her hotel and
wanders through the streets. The man follows her and asks her to stay
with him in Hiroshima. She thinks about it, but says no. She wanders
into a train station to rest. He follows her. She sits next to an old Japanese woman, and he rests on the other side of the old woman. She
places the past in perspective as she thinks to herself: "Three penny
romance. . . . I forget you here and now. One day without his eyes, and
she is ready to die. Little girl from Nevers, little tramp from Nevers.
One day without his hands, and she knows the tragedy of love. Little
girl of no account who died of love in Nevers. Little shorn head from
Nevers. I forget you here and now. Three penny romance."

Note how she talks of her young self in the third person. Instead
of saying, "It is cold when I'm in the cellar," she says, "She knows
the tragedy of love." She also calls her past affair a "three penny
romance," no longer an epic love, but an affair as common as those
found in the pulp magazines. She is finally living in the present. At
the same time, the man is also brought back to reality. It is the Japanese
woman who brings him out of his trance. Up to now, he has been
terribly involved with the woman and her story and could think of
nothing else. Now, the old woman speaks to him in Japanese, and he
answers, communicating, for the first time since the beginning of the
film, with someone other than his lover. Not only has he reestablished
communication with the "real world," but he has done so in his own
language.

In the meantime, the woman leaves the station unnoticed by her lover. She goes to a café, appropriately named Casablanca. It is likely the café is named for the movie, *Casablanca*, which has had an international impact. Through repeated showings, it has remained one of the principal forces in shaping our imaginative reconstruction of World War II and the issues involved in it. In this café, she lets a male stranger talk to her, very much the way it must have been with her lover a few nights before. She does not respond to the stranger. Her lover, on finding her in the café, sits at a different table, silently watching. This scene illustrates the final alienation between the man and woman. Dawn comes, and Resnais shows us shots of the New Hiroshima Hotel. In her room, the woman stands at the door, opens it, and the man enters. He says, "I could not stay away." She says, "I'll forget you; I already have; can't you see . . . look at me." Then she says, "Hiroshima . . . Hiroshima is your name." And he replies, "Yes, that is my name, and your name is Nevers . . . Nevers in France." The change that has taken place is complete. For the first time, these characters, nameless before so that they might portray every man and every woman, are named: Hiroshima and Nevers.

Resnais provides an ambiguous ending—the woman either remains with the man, or returns to France. She has, through the experience with her Japanese lover, relived her affair in Nevers. Now cured, she no longer needs her new love or her past love. What is important is that she is now different. She would like to see Nevers again—something she could never do before.

The film is a complex symbol system, made up of images, noises, words, and music. Resnais selects the audible symbols as carefully as the images. Snatches of sounds and different musical motifs all play a vital role—adding to the theme and communicating the film's meaning.

The film itself, though concerned with the destructive forces of war, is optimistic. The woman exorcises her past and is able to lead a new life. From the ashes, Hiroshima is rebuilt.

4

FRANK W. OGLESBEE

The World, the Flesh, and the Devil

Radiation became a major concern during the 1950s. Many "B" motion pictures presented an assortment of various radioactive animals—huge and menacing, primarily as a result of the effects of atomic fallout. Giant ants, mantises, grasshoppers, and snails prevailed; while other films offered unimaginative renditions of oversized humans. In this cinematic wasteland, an absence of science and an abundance of fiction prevailed. Although radioactive creatures are missing, similar scientific fancy and illogical behavior are apparent in Ranald Mac-Dougall's, *The World, the Flesh, and the Devil* (*WFD*). The film attempts to focus on both the struggle of surviving atomic war and solving racial conflicts. In 1959, most film critics agreed that although the initial scenes were impressive, the film's producers stretched their imaginations a great deal beyond their intellects.[1]

WFD begins with Ralph (Harry Belafonte) inspecting an abandoned mine tunnel; a cave-in abruptly seals him off from the rest of the world. Communicating with his fellow workers above, he requests help, but cannot hear incoming messages. Ralph settles down, confident of being rescued, eats lunch, and waits. After five days the digging stops. The cave's ceiling lights go out, and Ralph is forced to fend for himself by digging his way out. The irony of his entrapment becomes apparent, for the cave-in proves to be his salvation. The events correspond with his desire to emerge from subterranean darkness into the light, the allegorical journey from Hell.

Emerging from darkness, he discovers a deserted mine area, collided cars in the background, a pile of burning coal, and ominous silence. In the vacant office neither the phone nor radio works. A discarded newspaper carries headlines telling of retaliation for an atomic attack. An opened black umbrella sweeps past Ralph as he rushes homeward. The town is devoid of people.

An obvious strain of irony begins—civil defense posters, a sign warning that looters will be shot, and an emergency CD headquarters revealing only shiny white CD helmets. Here, the lack of CD effectiveness in dealing with massive war problems is suggested. A more blatant omission is obvious at this point; there is "no real intention of exploring the horror implicit in the situation."[2] While there are no live people, there are also no dead ones. In the more recent film, *The Omega Man*, victims are observed. But apparently, with *WFD* director-writer MacDougall decided to employ a special radioactive salt that both destroys and disintegrates human life.

Alone, Ralph decides to leave for New York, and like Charlton Heston in *The Omega Man*, he takes a new convertible from an auto dealer's showroom. The following scenes, bridges and tunnels of Manhattan blocked by vacant cars, the Statue of Liberty sans tourists, Ralph alone on a motorboat, effectively convey isolation. The camera then focuses on a CD poster, which reads, "Alert Today, Alive Tomorrow." Early-morning shots of a man alone in Manhattan are evocative illusions of desolation. Ralph rings a church bell, and as each peal sounds, the camera cuts from one animal monument to another. He enters a broadcasting station (CD posters again on the wall), where a tape recording reveals the past events. Interestingly, the emergency power supply is operable; the tape is cued and the power ready. Ralph learns that some unknown nation began the conflict by salting the atmosphere with radioactive sodium isotopes, emitting lethal doses for five days. Gradually, all other nations succumbed.

MacDougall's screenplay contends the world's inhabitants perished and vanished during the five days Ralph was underground. Is it entirely plausible that all nations used the same weapon within hours of each other? If the original attacker were unknown, who was retaliated against? Would five days be ample time for the radiation to cover the globe? In *On the Beach*, radiation from the northern hemisphere war took months to drift south and destroy Australia. How long must a person be exposed to radiation before dying? The realities of the situation are consistently not permitted to interfere with the contrivances.

Once Ralph gains control of the situation he locates supplies, a portable generator, and a Park Avenue apartment house. He finds two

The World, the Flesh, and the Devil. Courtesy of The Museum of Modern Art/Film Stills Archive

clothing store dummies for companionship (*The Omega Man* also used this device). By now, the audience realizes Ralph is not alone. A woman covertly watches him from around corners. Some weeks pass and the fixed smile of the male dummy becomes too much to bear. Ralph tosses it from the balcony. From a low-level shot, we first see the dummy hit the street, then the woman rushing toward it screaming. Ralph meets Sarah (Inger Stevens), who admits she has been following him for weeks, but was afraid to show herself. She has survived the fatal isotopes by remaining in a decompression chamber, while the others foolishly left it after two days.

Some explanation here would be useful—why did the others leave when she knew how long to stay? How did she avoid exposure to radiation when others opened the chamber door? Who ran the chamber's compressor for five days? Regrettably, audiences are asked to blindly accept the film's premise—it takes only a few days to destroy the world and for "normalcy" to return.

Ralph's varied expertise supplies gas for two automobiles, electricity for the buildings, radio programs, and efficient telephone service. He becomes a one-man staff of servants for Sarah. Sarah, however, requests equality. She does not wish Ralph to be her servant but rather a friend and even perhaps eventually her lover. She rejects his attempted aloofness by angrily saying, "I'm free, white and twenty-one and I can do what I please."

Throughout the film the relationship between the two lacks credibility. The dialogue is disappointingly shallow. One scene in particular illustrates this weakness. The two are lunching on Ralph's balcony. During the course of this pleasant tête-à-tête, they mention missing bread and fresh milk; yet if all the cows are dead, there will never again be fresh milk. The food-gathering problem in a postatomic age is ignored. It is as though there is an unlimited supply of edibles; obviously the radioactive salt has not penetrated canned goods.

Director MacDougall's three characters are the world, the flesh, and the devil. Ralph, mechanically inclined worker of the earth and keeper of the past, is the world. Sarah, warm, impulsive, nonintellectual, is the flesh. Prejudice could be the devil.

Ralph, as earth's symbol, eventually hears voices from Europe. He celebrates by having a birthday party for Sarah—a formal affair, replete with searchlights, tuxedo, nightclub, and recorded entertainment. When

Sarah again suggests a less formal arrangement, he mentions that there are other people.

Enter the devil; Ben (Mel Ferrer) arrives critically ill on a fishing boat. Ben has spent six months traveling—he has found no other survivors. How he survived is never mentioned. Ralph is able to save Ben's life, while Sarah carefully observes both men. A hopelessly banal romantic triangle begins.

The story now rapidly deteriorates. The three watch an old newsreel containing essentially innocuous material, which Ralph finds insignificant. His purpose in screening the newsreels was to ascertain what people had done before the war. Suddenly, Ben tells Ralph: "I have nothing against Negroes." The men's discussion degenerates into an argument about who should have the girl, thereby reducing the problem to the classical white myth about black men wanting white women. Overhearing the interchange, Sarah becomes annoyed—her right of choice is being ignored. Ben demands that she choose. She refuses. He decides to force the issue, suggesting that Ralph leave, but Ralph remains. The climax culminates in a shootout between Ben and Ralph.

MacDougall compounds this film cliché with a heavy-handed Gothic touch—a thunderstorm as a backdrop for the rivals' personal storm. (Is the dawn, when all again is calm, the dawn of reason?) Ralph, standing by a wall engraved with the old admonition of beating swords into plowshares, throws away his weapon. Ben cannot shoot. Ralph turns to leave, only to be stopped by Sarah, who asks him to stay. They run to Ben, and as the film concludes, they walk off hand in hand. The closing title reads, "The Beginning." Then, instead of symbolic doves, New York pigeons appear. Radiation apparently has not affected them.

In conclusion, critic Paul Beckley considered the film "enthralling," and wrote, "the solution seems logical enough."[3] Most other reviewers found the film unsatisfactory. *Time* called it, "monumentally silly," as did the *Monthly Film Bulletin*.[4] Unfortunately, the two problems of race relations and radiation war were not properly examined. The film is no better than Roger Corman's "B" movie, *The Last Woman on Earth* (1960), which also incorporated a triangle love story into the aftermath of an atomic holocaust, with two men competing for the favor of the final surviving woman. As with *WFD*, Corman's film is unrealistic, asking viewers to accept a scenario in which all living things, with the exception of three characters, die as atomic dust passes over an island. The three survive only because they were deep-sea diving and wearing special aqualungs.

Of *WFD*'s ending, Bosley Crowther said: "so cozily theatrical that you wouldn't be surprised to see the windows of buildings suddenly crowded with reintegrated people, cheering happily and flinging ticker tape."[5] Of its approach to the race problem, critic Albert Johnson believed that *WFD* "exemplifies today's approach to the theme of interracialism—vague, inconclusive, and undiscussed."[6] Not all films concerned with black-white relationships could claim such honor. The films of the 1950s which best treat the subject of race relations are *Edge of the City* and *The Defiant Ones*. They are less than ideal, but much better than *WFD*. As Hollis Alpert wrote, "Segregationist Southerners and the South African government will be heartened to know that even in a relatively empty world the race problem continues."[7]

The only credible moments in *The World, the Flesh, and the Devil* result from Harold Mazroati's serene cinematography, and the cast's valiant attempts to overcome the material. The foreboding landscapes, as captured by Mazroati's disciplined composition, serve as a memorable apocalyptic sermon. Cinematically, the aftermath of the bomb, as presented in *WFD*, is an artistic achievement. But overall, *WFD* is a disappointing, unimaginative, and unreasonable view of the problems of race and nuclear war.

5

JOSEPH KEYERLEBER

On the Beach

When Stanley Kramer's *On the Beach* was released in 1959, it was accompanied by great fanfare and received substantial critical comment. It was lauded as a deterrent to further nuclear armament. *Saturday Review*, commenting on its simultaneous release in world capitals, announced that "it can only do good." Scientist Linus Pauling said, "It may be that some years from now we can look back and say that *On the Beach* is the movie that saved the world." *New York Times* critic Bosley Crowther wrote: "The basic theme of this drama and its major concern is life, the wondrous thing that man's own knowledge and ultimate folly seem to destroy. And everything done by the characters, every thought they utter and move they make, indicates their fervor, tenacity and courage in the face of doom. . . . The great merit of this film, aside from its entertaining qualities, is the fact that it carries a passionate conviction that man is worth saving after all. Life is a beautiful treasure and man should do all he can to save it from annihilation while there is still time." [1]

But *On the Beach*, although possessing unwavering concern for life, is a film of overwhelming nondistinction. It achieved international acclaim primarily because it was an extensive film-making effort concerned with historical and contemporary dimensions of the nuclear dilemma. At the time of its release, paranoid fear of nuclear war gripped the world. The film merited some critical recognition, primarily because of its timely topic—certain death for the world's remaining survivors reflects the complete annihilation of all mankind. The helplessness of man theme, while awaiting slow poisoning caused by radioactive fallout, is depicted in a candid and awesome manner. Yet the film, writes John Howard Lawson, cannot escape the contradiction between the greatness of its theme and the lack of depth in its treatment. Although Kramer's direction is thoughtful and honest, he does not scale the heights of human experience. "His ideas," notes Lawson, "never go beneath the surface of events."[2]

Arthur Knight praised the film: "The point of growing up is facing up—facing up to the problems and issues of our times and our society. And in this Stanley Kramer stands alone among Hollywood producers today. . . . *On the Beach* is a film that aims at something big and emerges as something tremendous."[3] Knight makes the mistake of attempting to offer social criticism and fails to discuss the relative attributes of this production in terms of film artistry. Instead, he philosophizes on the ending (a Salvation Army banner proclaiming, "There is still time, Brother"; it flaps in the wind over a town square devoid of life). In San Francisco, the audience laughed during the scene, but to Knight, "It is at once a reminder and a warning, giving meaning to the entire story."[4]

Time magazine, in characteristic style, offered a different evaluation: "a sentimental sort of radical romance in which the customers are spared any scenes of realistic horror, and are asked instead to accept the movie notion of what is really horrible about the end of the world: boy (Gregory Peck) does not get girl (Ava Gardner). Aside from its sentimentality, the worst of the film's offenses is its reality. Though Kramer and company predict that *On the Beach* will act 'as a deterrent to further nuclear armaments,' the picture actually manages to make the most dangerous conceivable situation in human history seem rather silly and science-fictional. The players look half-dead long before the fallout gets them. But what could any actors make of a script that imagines the world's end as a scene in which Ava Gardner stands and wistfully waves goodbye as Gregory Peck sails sadly into the contaminated dawn."[5]

Perhaps some historical perspective of the times may illustrate why the release of *On the Beach* was a cause for celebration. The film appeared during the peak of cold war paranoia in the United States. Nuclear war with Russia seemed a very real possibility that, if it took place, would surely lead to total global destruction. *Life* magazine referred to teen-agers as the Silent Generation, disaffected, disenchanted, and disinterested because of the pervading sense of insecurity; building bomb shelters was good business at the time. Upon reflection,

On the Beach. Courtesy of The Museum of Modern Art/Film Stills Archive

we notice Americans were primed psychologically for *On the Beach*, the first major motion picture to deal with the theme of nuclear world war. As inadequate as the film may now seem, in 1959 it did promote concern and caused many to reflect. As film producer-director Stanley Kramer contends: "I take a very dim view as to the ultimate effect of a single film on the spectator. I don't think it can change anyone's mind."[6] Kramer does not attempt to change viewpoints; he tries to provoke viewers to think about situations and to look at them in a way in which they did not see them before.

Kramer has no illusions about his popularity. Because his films are controversial, he contends half the people will disagree with him. When he was making *On the Beach*, even the scientists he consulted were divided on the question of whether or not, in the event of a nuclear holocaust, the world would be totally destroyed. He also encountered difficulties with the United States government; his request to borrow a nuclear submarine was turned down by the State Department. The assistant secretary of state disagreed with Kramer's thesis that a nuclear war would wipe out civilization. The official stated that if a holocaust should occur there would only be "eight or nine million casualties."[7]

Today, perhaps we seem less fearful of mushroom-shaped clouds looming on the horizon, less susceptible to manipulation of our emotions. We can more easily analyze *On the Beach* for what it is: a $4 million soap opera endeavoring to qualify as cinematic art, merely because it is concerned with an important topic. The outlook of the film, however, is psychologically and artistically structured by commercial restrictions; the result is a lucrative venture masquerading as social consciousness.

On the Beach is an excellent example of the Stanley Kramer formula for successful film making: combine a theme of great social significance with an expensive cast of superstars and the final product subsequently brings profit and prestige to the producer-director. Although Kramer was satisfied the film was produced, he was also probably aware of its shortcomings. These weaknesses may be found in many feature film productions of the 1950s: staginess and wooden actors. There are also obvious production mistakes. The process shots of the Australian Grand Prix Race sequence—Fred Astaire sits in his Ferrari on the studio set with the track projected behind him—are not realistic. Throughout the film, Kramer carefully establishes a gasoline shortage. He then conveniently provides Astaire and his fellow racers with an abundant supply of petrol for the Grand Prix. Additionally, while others use horse-drawn carriages, Ava Gardner drives a convertible and Gregory Peck is chauffeured in a Rolls-Royce.

As with most Hollywood nuclear features, *On the Beach* employs several romantic episodes to convey a more horrible reality. First, a young navy lieutenant (Anthony Perkins) and his wife (Donna Anderson) have difficulty coping with impending death. He has no illusions about the end and wants his wife and child to die painlessly. She refuses to accept the inevitable. Second, Capt. Dwight Lionel Towers (Gregory Peck), whose family has since perished in the United States, is paired with Moira Davidson (Ava Gardner). Moira's love is rejected by the captain; he continually speaks of his family as though they are still alive. Third, Moira seeks consolation from her former lover, Julian (Fred Astaire). Julian, a cynical scientist who helped develop the bomb, prefers the exhilaration of auto racing. Finally, a crusty Australian navy admiral incessantly barks out orders to his attractive, young secretary, Osgood.

Lieutenant Holmes eventually guides his wife to reason. He admits he loves her; she confesses she has been foolish and impractical. When Captain Towers admits he loves Moira, it is too late. Julian, on winning the Grand Prix, commits suicide by asphyxiating himself in his Ferrari. The admiral and his secretary share a final toast of sherry. On asking if she has any young beaux, she replies, "no." He comments, "Blind world."

The treatment of the dialogue is generally cliché. For example, when the lieutenant's wife hosts a cocktail party, Julian becomes philosophical, explaining that nuclear war was not an accident. "The world was probably destroyed by a handful of vacuum tubes and transistors" he observes; "the guilt is not on scientists or motherhood." The lieutenant's wife breaks down melodramatically. She hysterically argues, "I won't have it. There *is* hope. There has to be hope. We can't go on like this."

At times, however, the seriousness of Nevil Shute's novel is convincingly adapted. Shute wrote of a civilization that deliberately created a device for its own destruction. In the novel, one of his protagonists articulates the dilemma: "I don't know. . . . Some kinds of silliness you can't stop . . . if a couple of hundred million people all decide that their national honour requires them to drop cobalt bombs upon their neighbour, well, there's not much that you or I can do about it. The only

possible hope would have been to educate them out of their silliness."[8]
Thus, some dramatic subject matter is transferred to the screen, making
the film suitably interesting and maintaining the viewer's attention.

Occasionally, *On the Beach* approaches film artistry. Several scenes
offer poignant impressions which remind the viewer that the film is
more than a love story. Lieutenant Holmes is commissioned to serve
aboard the *Sawfish* as liaison officer. Julian assists as a civilian scientific
advisor. Directed by Captain Towers, the *Sawfish* sails as far north as
Alaska to determine whether radioactive fallout will reach Australia.
On the return of their thirteen-thousand mile reconnaissance mission,
they examine American West Coast cities to assess the effects and try
to locate a transmitter that has sent out intermittent, nonsensical messages. An inspection is made of San Francisco. The vessel passes
under a completely vacant Golden Gate Bridge. Within viewing range
of the city, the periscope scans a metropolis deprived of its vitality. A
cacophony accompanies each scene that is revealed: empty, lifeless
streets, dormant docks. The crew members are profoundly affected. A
yeoman abandons ship to die in his home city.

The *Sawfish* continues to seek the source of the mysterious radio
transmissions. While trying to feign skepticism, the men cling to a hope
there may still be an outpost of civilization in the Northern Hemisphere.
The messages continue. Signals indicate the source is somewhere near
San Diego. On arrival, one crew member is sent out to investigate in a
protective suit. He walks through empty refineries; the musical score
taps out a Morse-code rhythm. He finds a well-identified "POWER
HOUSE," and examines its functioning hydroelectric generators. A
short walk leads him to the radio room and its crushing revelation.
Relating the intelligence of its extinct creators, the crewman opens the
key and taps out, "window shade tugging on a Coke bottle." He closes
down the transmitter, shuts off the generators, and makes his way back
to the submarine. There are no remaining illusions that the extinction
may not be complete—it is and will be.

Kramer intertwines some honest moments of satire as comic relief in
On the Beach. A spoof on role-playing recurs. "It's all due to the wine
committee," bemoan two stodgy old gentlemen, seated in an exclusive
club. Their only problem, as the world approaches its end, is how to
consume four hundred bottles of wine. They continually badger the
maître d' to bring additional bottles and glasses. Kramer uses this trivial
fretting to emphasize an ironic twist—it is the harassed waiter who

survives. In the deserted clubroom, he pours a glass of the vintage wine, takes a sip, picks up a billiard cue, and shoots. Suddenly, the lights go out, a symbolic indication the end is near.

One conceptually disturbing aspect of the film was the willingness of people to take government-issued suicide pills. Doctors distributed packets of Government Prescription No. 24768 to an all-too-eager public. One scene shows Captain Towers observing a long line of recipients waiting patiently. Trying to conceal emotion, he directs his chauffeur onward. The pills were intended to prevent prolonged suffering from radiation sickness. However logical this might have been under the circumstances, it hardly indicates "fervor, tenacity and courage in the face of doom." The natural drive for survival and the strength of the human spirit should cause some if not many people to refuse to accept the painless way out. *On the Beach* almost casually accepts the notion that once radiation sickness comes, there is nothing to do but relax and die.

Two elements of film production are notable. There is an absorbing musical score by Ernest Gold; he unifies dramatic sequences with skillful variations on the theme of the Australian folk song, "Waltzing Matilda." Giuseppe Rotunno's excellent black and white photography creates vivid and trenchant images, subtly impressing the viewer; man ashore in the deserted city of San Francisco, the waste of a world devoid of people is contrasted with Australia's remaining citizens behaving in an almost normal fashion. Thus, the imagined annihilation of all mankind becomes both an injection of realism and fantasy due to the sharp probing of Rotunno's sensitive imagery.[9]

As Moira and Julian, Ava Gardner and Fred Astaire perform capably, while Anthony Perkins and Donna Anderson, as Lieutenant and Mrs. Holmes are also suitably convincing. In the role of Captain Towers, Gregory Peck, as meticulous and imaginative a performer as he is, was not given ample opportunity to distinguish himself. His actions were restricted and predetermined, offering only fragmented responses to analytical phrases of dialogue.

In discussing *On the Beach*, critic John Lawson says of Kramer: "He deserves credit for maintaining the moral integrity of the American film at a time when the main policies of the industry deny moral values and dishonor art. . . . The hatred of war which motivates *On the Beach* must be contrasted to the glorification of war in other films."[10] The film presented a liberal viewpoint, seen in terms of its period. This is in retrospect, however; because when seen now, it is rather weak due to the lack of depth, passion, and characterization, but also because of the progressive tempo of the nuclear arms race. When Nevil Shute's *On the Beach* was published, only three nations possessed nuclear weapons. With today's nuclear situation, Kramer's version of the Shute text, though initially impressive, is greatly diminished.

6 MARK HALL

The Day the Earth
Caught Fire

The view of the future, as witnessed in *The Day the Earth Caught Fire*, produced and directed by Val Guest, is horrifying because it is the logical extension of an illogical present. The film relates what may happen if the Soviet Union and the United States exploded simultaneous nuclear tests, changing the earth's slant toward the sun. *Fire*'s plot progresses slowly; it is almost half an hour before we discover what has gone wrong. Then we are shown London (and presumably the world) being thwarted by a series of "natural" calamities. Like the plagues of the Old Testament, each incident is more dangerous, more threatening as the world slowly dies a painful death.

One often sees the future in terms of how one sees his world. If afraid now, he will be frightened of the future. In a science-fiction film, he is asked to accept somebody else's perception of the future based on *his* feeling toward his present.

Since science-fiction films are primarily concerned with the effects of science on man, it is natural that their themes would be related to the technology available when the film was made. Science-fiction films from the late thirties, such as *Flash Gordon Goes to Mars*, appear out of date today. Technological awareness has caught up with and surpassed the movie predictions of forty years ago; it is a case of reality catching up with fantasy.

I can remember coming home from the Saturday matinees of my youth, my mind reeling with the possibilities of inventing a serum to make me invisible. After all, if Bela Lugosi could invent a death ray, I certainly could whip together a potion to turn me transparent. I learned about experimentation from the movies. I learned when you start mixing substances together, sometimes strange results occur. It was through science-fiction films I first learned of the possibilities of chemistry, physics, and engineering. Science-fiction movies, and the exploits of "mad" scientists who lived in that reality, provided models. But, more importantly, I had a feeling of excitement that far overshadowed anything in a school science text. The dreams of movie scientists, with their mysterious but wonderously complex mountain laboratories, somehow became the dreams, perhaps unconscious dreams, of today's scientists.

Until the bomb was dropped, science-fiction writers had little but imaginary material with which to work; they generated stories about natural calamities, space travel, and the like, since their imagination was limited by the availability of technology. The atomic age solved the problem and has since provided a never-ending stream of themes for science-fiction movies. When the bomb was exploded, we saw our first glimpse of the end of the world. For the first time, we became aware we could destroy the entire planet. We have never really recovered from that shock. The hysteria over the potential danger of atomic warfare has been tempered in recent years, as we have learned to live under the shadow of technological annihilation.

During the early 1950s, our concern about atomic annihilation was very apparent. The mass media contained numerous stories relating the effects of atomic radiation, the latest pictures of the atomic bomb tests, and plans for building backyard bomb shelters. We seemed ready for an atomic war, but nothing happened. Our fear became less a part of our daily lives as we realized that even if the bomb was dropped, there was little we could do. The bomb is an ominous instrument of destruction—the end of the world. What will happen if the bomb is dropped? We do not know, so we look for answers.

In the fifteen years between 1950 and 1965, the science-fiction movie was a catalogue of possible results of atomic warfare, either by accident or design. Interwoven into the "fear of the bomb" motif was concern about the effects of atomic radiation on living organisms. Countless monster science-fiction motion pictures, from *Them* to *Godzilla*, dwelled on future disasters.

The number of these films produced since World War II is staggering. One of the weakest is *Damnation Alley* (1977), which features

The Day the Earth Caught Fire. Courtesy of *Movie Star News*

floods, tornadoes, explosions, and hordes of armor-plated killer cock-roaches. One of the best is a "bomb-fear" science-fiction film, Val Guest's *The Day the Earth Caught Fire*, produced by British Lion Films in 1961. Unlike most science-fiction films, *Fire* was bereft of spectacular machines and explosions expected in this type of film or genre. Perhaps that is why the film was never a commercial success—it simply did not live up to our preconceptions.

This lack of spectacle may have made it a better film because it presented a more realistic view of the future. The objects shown in the film—cars, houses, clothing, life styles, people—were realistic because of their familiarity. The more probable the view of a science-fiction movie, the more impact that film is likely to have. The film's probability is directly related to how easy it is to make the mental move from the present to the future. If the step is too great, if the movie asks for an acceptance of numerous changes, if it is arduous to believe, the film should not be taken seriously. If a science-fiction film includes enough of the familiar, if there are sufficient scenes of the present in the fictional future, it may be taken seriously. *Fire* belongs in the latter category. The world of *Fire* is a world one could accept if one awoke and discovered something had gone wrong following an atomic blast—a very real possibility. The film is set in the "present." The clothing, furniture, streets, and people are contemporary. More impor-tantly, the day-to-day routine of the screen characters is an accurate mirror, reflecting current life-styles. There is little difference between the actions and activities shown in the film and "normal" life experi-ences. The bridge between "now" and the "future" is very narrow, so narrow, that it is easy to make the mental stride into "tomorrow."

To deal with today's technological problems, science fiction must have a sense of urgency. The future we are asked to consider is very close to the present, so close at times it may be hard to tell the dif-ferences between science fiction and reality.

By 1960, for example, the awesome threat of nuclear war was easing in the minds of many. Years had passed as we hovered on the proverbial brink, and by now there was somewhat of a lull in the testing of nu-clear weapons, increasing pressure to stop these tests, and it seemed as if the world might be becoming a safer place to live in.

Then, in 1961, an attempt by the United States to "liberate" Cuba resulted in the creation of the Berlin Wall by the Soviet Union. Subsequently, a resumption of nuclear testing by the Soviets took place (followed by the United States), in which the Russians set off a hydrogen test bomb three hundred times stronger than the Hiroshima devastator. It was during this time of crisis that *Fire* was released. A twentieth-century morality play, the film challenges the right of few to endanger many. It also focuses on individual isolation and alienation, while capturing fear of the unknown over which man has no control.

Told from the outlook of an alcoholic has-been reporter for the London *Daily Express* (Edward Judd), the story offers a pessimistic view of the future. After Judd makes his final report to the press room, the film unfolds as a flashback. It begins slowly with a detailed character sketch of the protagonist (a divorcé with a small child he dearly loves, in the custody of his ex-wife) and a definition of the people's "right to know," as stated in the policy of the *Daily Express*. The seriousness of the dialogue and the honesty of intentions are immediately apparent.

As the plot begins to develop, we learn the United States and Soviet Russia have simultaneously and coincidentally detonated 50-megaton hydrogen test bombs; one at the North Pole and the other at the South Pole. Thus begins an intensive research and reporting task by the *Express*, to investigate potential results of these blasts, in order to bring them to the attention of the people—much to the dismay of national politicians.

Here, the film's love interest blossoms, as the hero develops a sudden convenient interest in a government switchboard operator. The operator (Janet Munro), becomes his contact because, "surely she must have heard something." He eventually discovers the government is withholding information from the public concerning an eleven-degree shift in the earth's angle of rotation caused by the simultaneous blasts. Government officials balk at releasing the information; they wait, refusing to confirm stories printed in the *Express*. The newspaper reveals the earth's orbit is on a collision course with the sun. The government remains silent.

It is not until a heat wave followed by a drought and severe water shortage, forcing rationing and public baths, that officials decide to comfort the populace with the well-worn "there is nothing to be alarmed about." The tension is intensified by Les Bowie's professional special effects—a heavy, dank mist that covers London, and a raging cyclone that virtually destroys sections of the city. The effects are shockingly realistic.

By now, hysteria is beginning to grip the city (and the world). People begin to riot out of fear and frustration, while forced hardships are brought on by events beyond their control. The delayed delivery of unbelievable truth, as disseminated by the media, has created havoc. In one scene, a group of disenchanted youths, ignoring government regulations, steals a water truck and begins an epic orgy in water. Their mindless frenzy is perhaps indicative of events of the time.

By the film's conclusion, all the powers have united (as they usually do in science-fiction Armageddon adventures). They simultaneously fire four nuclear bombs placed near the equator, in an attempt to correct the disaster they have created by their own negligence. The film ends on a scene in the press room of two distribution-ready copies of the *Daily Express*, one bearing the headline "Earth Saved!" and the other, "Earth Doomed." The decision, then, is for the viewer to make the choice of an ending, as the hero walks off into the sunset to discover the results of the blasts for himself.

Despite some commercialized love interest in the film (it received an X rating from the British Board of Censors), most likely added to increase its salability, and the sometimes unconvincing special effects, *Fire* is a striking characterization of the early atomic age.

To some, the film may say that presently we have a chance to avoid a holocaust by working together. (This theme is also apparent in the British film, *Crack in the World* [1965]; here scientists cooperate by using nuclear bombs to save the earth. Both films serve as a moral reminder that we cannot refuse to accept the responsibility for our actions.) But to others, *Fire* says, "the world will end with a whimper, not a bang." The vast majority of us die quietly, unnoticed in the mainstream of humanity.

Fire suggests that most of us may dismiss the possibility of atomic warfare, believing our leaders are sufficiently intelligent to prevent total annihilation. The nuclear arms race is accepted as technological sword-rattling, as international, scientific, "mine is bigger than yours" game-playing. Forecasting an all-too-real future, Val Guest's *Fire*, unlike many of its counterparts, does not end on an optimistic note. The death throes are not necessarily halted and normality is not restored. If our planet does face atomic extinction, it will most probably not be as the result of a planned exercise in nuclear warfare. *Fire* is frightening because of the possibility it may be real. We might learn of atomic error as we crunch cold cereal and our eyes rove to an obscure article on the back pages. As the days pass, the same article may find its way to the paper's front page. As it grows in importance, so too will our awareness, but it may be too late.

7

JACK G. SHAHEEN

Panic in Year Zero

Panic in Year Zero is a melodramatic story about a typical middle-class family and their reactions following an atomic holocaust. Given the film's premise, what occurs is generally predictable. The film contains trite philosophical handwringing about civilization, love, and survival. It is interesting, however, for its philosophical naïveté, and as a window back to those years when *Life* magazine was printing instructions on how to build bomb shelters in backyards. Since *Panic in Year Zero* is so entwined with American mythology of the sixties, it merits investigation.

Harry Baldwin (Ray Milland) and his wife Ann (Jean Hagen) are a stereotyped all-American family with two teen-agers, Rick (Frankie Avalon) and Karen (Mary Mitchell), off on a two-week vacation. Suddenly, en route to their summer camp, they discover atomic bombs have been dropped over Los Angeles, destroying their home and loved ones. Harry immediately decides the greatest danger facing his family is not radioactive fallout but hordes of potential looters, among them a trio of young toughs who are ravaging the countryside. He offers a self-survival plan, which emulates the every-man-for-himself theme. Everyone listens to dad and obeys him. Women's liberation does not exist. This is an accurate reflection of the way in which early-sixties women's magazines, such as *Family Circle* and *Ladies Home Journal*, stressed the importance of the family unit. Togetherness was the prevalent theme with dad as leader.

Their journey for survival also takes on religious significance. Harry recognizes the trip as a second Exodus, a search for truth in the wilderness. In one scene containing biblical overtones, he parts a stream of

Panic in Year Zero. Courtesy of The Museum of Modern Art/Film Stills Archive

cars blocking the family's escape by pouring gasoline over the road and setting it on fire. Unlike Moses, Harry was not waiting for a miracle; his is the religion of survival. Uttering the film's dominant theme, Harry says, "We can start with one basic fact—us."

For a complacent middle-class family man, he quickly adjusts to the newly created jungle. He robs a hardware store when he cannot pay the bill and knocks out a service station attendant in order to have sufficient gas. Rick emulates his father; he totes a shotgun boasting: "We are on our own, Ma. No rules, regulations or laws." Such is the film's attempt at morality; it is unintentionally embarrassing.

The mother's role is nearly nonexistent, her principal function in the film is to occasionally counterpoint the moral disintegration of the men. Dubiously, she represents love, goodness, Christian morality, and civilization; and in retrospect, a typical treatment of women in disaster films.

Panic occasionally focuses on character development—Harry struggles to accept Ann's Christian ideals, while she correspondingly becomes an advocate of the gun. Conflicting moral philosophies collide when her daughter is raped. The direction of the rape scene and its subsequent reverberations is unpleasant and vacuous.

During the rape sequence, underscored by Les Baxter's racy, abrasive rock and roll music, Ann wanders on the scene, discovers what is happening, and immediately tries to shoot the two assailants. Her Christian attitude abruptly changes; she will kill, if necessary, to save her daughter. This is a realistic gesture, unlike the violent reactions of the men, who are constantly in search of potential victims. Whatever point the film had intended to make by focusing on the mother's conversion to her husband's belief in violence is lost, due to the incompatibility of the two situations. Ann's honest reaction to the attack on her daughter, as compared to Harry's obsession with violence, is unsatisfactory.

Harry and Rick eventually hunt down the two rapists and shoot them at close range. Finding a young girl the rapists had kidnapped, they meaningfully decide to offer assistance in lieu of committing murder. Harry justifies his actions: "I looked for the worst in others and I found it in myself." He comes by this philosophy rather belatedly.

Panic concludes with a return to civilized morals. The typical film solution for a new beginning is young love. Rick and the rescued girl, Marilyn (Joan Freeman), immediately begin exchanging inquiring glances. Rick gives her his best smile; they explore the woods for his rabbit traps. Suddenly the lone remaining member of the gang appears. To save Rick, Marilyn takes the intruder's rifle and kills him. Rick, however, is seriously wounded.

Humanistic technology is then introduced by a country doctor. The physician, who had been previously terrorized by raging crowds, decides to save Rick and thus the future of mankind. Characteristically, Harry recognizes the larger meaning here; he gratefully tells the doctor: "You know, watching you work is like raising your head up out of the mud and slime and seeing civilization again. I thought we'd lost it for good." Civilization and the hope of mankind return. The film, for the first and only time, suggests technology may be used for humanistic ends; technology is not evil at all; it is neutral. If man builds bombs or guns, that is bad; if he makes scalpels, that is good.

Panic obviously portends that society cannot survive under the aegis of perpetual barbarism; civilization is possible only by law, order, and faith in the younger generation. When the radio reports Los Angeles is safe from looting and fallout, the Baldwin family and Marilyn anticipate civilization will soon be renewed again, perhaps for the better this time. The restraints of formal law and communications will return. In what is unintended sardonic humor, the film ends with the survivors reaching safety. Ann sees the United States Army and humbly thanks God. The camera focuses on two soldiers—

PRIVATE: That's five more.
SERGEANT: Five more what?
PRIVATE: Five more that are OK. They came from the hills. No radiation sickness.
SERGEANT: Yep, . . . five more good ones.

Fade out slowly. Bring up stirring music and full capital insert—

THERE MUST BE NO END

ONLY A NEW BEGINNING

Panic in Year Zero attempts to analyze the kinds of human consciousness that follow atomic war. It demonstrates that civilization's neurosis is begotten by technology. The result, unfortunately, is not critically analyzed; the film purports to offer an easy philosophy of becoming barbaric to survive. It attempts to show a chilling view of man's darker side but never rises beyond an all-too-typical surface view, using stereotyped characters that are never given a chance to reveal genuine depth or development. *Panic* consistently loops back on itself—the new beginning is the old belief in technology and the ethos of the gun. The film is a bleak unrealistic manual on how to survive in a postatomic war atmosphere. It does little to dignify and interpret for audiences the nuclear issue. Instead, *Panic*'s misleading and superficial theme functions only as a means of distortion and exaggeration.

8

RAMEY ELLIOT AND JACK G. SHAHEEN

Ladybug, Ladybug

Most nuclear war films are concerned with several questions: should the bomb be dropped; if it is on the way, how can it be stopped; how may nuclear holocausts be prevented; and at what level should critical decisions be made. The common theme linking these films is a command decision made by those individuals or groups who possess the authority to release nuclear weapons. The drama of the films centers primarily on high-level decisions and individual characterizations, usually people with power who are not risking their own lives, but rather the fate of millions.

Another type of nuclear war film is *Ladybug, Ladybug*, not to be confused with the popular children's nursery rhyme. Here, the action centers on a group of schoolchildren in a peaceful rural community, and their reactions to a sudden threatened bomb attack. The Frank and Eleanor Perry film exemplifies the emotional turmoil of the victims of *possible* nuclear attack, there is no consideration given to government decisions or military operations.

The plot of *Ladybug, Ladybug* centers on the plight of elementary schoolchildren sent home during a nuclear alert. The drama is constructed, in this case, through the children's relationships with their teachers, parents, and each other, and the way they emotionally behave, knowing imminent annihilation is feasible. The Perrys' group of schoolchildren appears to be a microcosm, reflecting attitudes and emotions toward nuclear war that existed during the Cuban missile crisis of the sixties. Their attitudes and emotions reveal apathy, pessimism, disbelief, lack of understanding, religious fervor, greed, selfishness, heroism, and jealousy. While this wide range of attitudes could be effectively presented, the film fails in attempting to explore too many areas, in lieu of concentrating on selected action.

Ladybug, Ladybug opens with the sound of an alert; the yellow light flashes as the warning system's constant buzzing permeates the school's office area, creating feelings of fear and confusion. The school secretary checks out the alarm code—nuclear attack imminent within one hour. Unable to make a decision, she calls the principal. They want to believe the alarm is false, but they express overwhelming feelings of insecurity and doubt. The principal, failing to receive assurances of safety from the telephone company (he is told by the operator that all seven areas of the system must go wrong before the phone company can consider the possibility of a malfunction), eventually decides to send everyone home. Although the attack may occur within sixty minutes, there is no panic; nor is there consideration given to the possibility of using the school as a shelter. The building is evacuated and the children are placed in selected groups. Some take the only bus while the majority begin walking home with their teachers. As they depart, the school secretary laments, "It may not be a drill, we don't know yet. We can't get anyone on the phone." The principal, responding to her anxiety, states, "I'm going to get on that phone and stay on it until I get somebody." This conflict, pessimism versus optimism, pervaded the late fifties and early sixties, and is the essence of the film's dramatic content.

As a subaspect of the pessimism-optimism struggle, the Perrys introduce only two situations in which people seek answers and hope for survival. Luke, one of the schoolchildren, for example, goes home and begins stocking the cellar with provisions; he is confronted by his senile grandmother who thinks he is playing another game. Luke, realizing he cannot reason with her, is unable to make her understand what is about to happen because he himself does not understand. There is only one way to have both supplies and grandmother in the cellar—he convinces her that she should play the game, "Hide from War." The game, of course, is to play at escaping from war caused by villains. To escape from war is an impossibility, and the enemy an abstraction. Similarly, two other schoolmates, Don and Trudy, explain to their mother what is happening; she immediately rushes them to the basement. There they begin praying for protection from the bomb. Don then asks his mother: who made the bad men? Did God make the bomb? The Perrys focus on these two episodes, not with the intention of providing adequate

Ladybug, Ladybug. Courtesy of Swank Motion Pictures, Inc.

answers, but to reveal the existing fear that prevailed at the time their film was produced.

The main story line is dominated by three primary characters, Sarah, Steve, and Harriet. They form a juvenile puppy-love triangle that has disastrous results. Sarah is depicted as the sweet girl next door, and Steve, the boy next door; Harriet is viewed as the rich, spoiled, selfish brat whose family owns a deluxe fallout shelter.

Following the sounding of the alert, Harriet offers to share the shelter with selected friends; Steve and his brother join her. During the walk home the children move rather slowly, singing, reciting rhymes and playing various games; there is no hurry to reach safety until arrival at the shelter. Here an abrupt behavioral change occurs. They become emotional and frightened of the bomb threat. (In the early sixties, the Russians were considered to be the most feared enemy, yet no mention is made as to who might be dropping the bomb.) The children begin emulating the actions of adults. When Harriet and her group retreat into the shelter, duties are immediately assigned. Each child is given some responsibility; sleeping hours and guard duties are declared, while food and water become rationed. Harriet is in command because it is her shelter.

Meanwhile, Sarah has taken Don and Trudy to their mother. On reaching her home, Sarah finds an empty house and panics. No explanation is offered as to why Sarah does not seek refuge in her own dwelling or in Don and Trudy's home, which is nearby. Instead, she runs through an open field and garbage area, all the way back to Harriet's shelter. Although Steve protests, Harriet refuses to allow Sarah to enter. There isn't enough food or water, she says; with an extra person the air won't last; there's no room; it's my shelter. Harriet, obviously jealous of Sarah, is a "have"; Sarah, a "have-not." Harriet is willing to do away with Sarah, indirectly, to gain Steve.

In desperation, Sarah runs blindly in search of protection. She discovers an old refrigerator in the junkyard (which symbolically suggests what the earth might resemble after an atomic attack) and closes the door, with full knowledge of the results. Steve tries to find her but is literally scared senseless by a military jet flying overhead, which he mistakes for an attack plane. The film concludes on his screaming. Harriet and her select group are shown as "chosen survivors," and an insecure Luke and his grandmother lie huddled in an unsafe cellar, while Don and Trudy are seen praying. Perhaps this unsatisfactory conclusion reflects the Perrys' thesis concerning nuclear war—no resolution is feasible. Although the alert turns out to be a false alarm, it is too late for Sarah. What remains is the Perrys' intention—a pessimistic vision of human behavior under the stress of nuclear attack.

The false alert as drama is also employed in Alfred E. Green's *Invasion U.S.A.* (1953). Green's film, however, focuses on adult behavior. It also relies almost entirely on stock World War II combat footage that graphically shows an impending nuclear holocaust. Unlike *Ladybug, Ladybug, Invasion* offers an optmistic vision of human behavior. Under stress, Green's adults lose their complacency and become militaristic. Whereas the Perrys' conclusion is ambiguous, Green's is concise; during the final frames his protagonists rush to turn tractor factories into tank plants.[1]

Ladybug, Ladybug's technical standards are high and the symbolism is effective. As with other Perry films, *David and Lisa, Last Summer*, and *Trilogy*, the symbolism is expressed not with dialogue but with appropriate music and precise character movements. In an impressive symbolic antiwar sequence, the Perrys, ably assisted by Robert Cobert's haunting musical score (featuring successive tones of harp, piano, and oboe), show the school secretary tidying up the children's play area. She is alone. In the sandbox, a cannon stands atop a play fortress. She hastily buries the toy, replacing its implied threat (death) with models of a man and woman with child (life). Here the music abruptly ceases. Word arrives—it is a false alarm caused by "some sort of short circuit." For the time being, the Perrys suggest, man will survive.

The basic concept of placing children, instead of adults, in a situation in which they face imminent death, can create good drama. The problem the Perrys encounter with *Ladybug, Ladybug*, in both writing and direction, is in ascribing very adult attitudes to children. Steve's classmate, whose father is an engineer, knowingly says a bomb cannot destroy a good shelter, "unless it's a direct hit." In another scene the children, especially the boys, discuss the terrifying consequences of Hiroshima and war. Concerning the morality of dropping the bomb, Harriet confidently asserts, "It wouldn't be my fault if it was an order."

Most children love to play at war and to kill the imagined enemy. It was not an uncommon sight in the early sixties to see a boy carrying toy knives, grenades, rifles, and submachine guns. Boys were attracted to army jeeps that featured "atomic brakes." Toy atomic bombs were available and added to the play arsenal.

Writer Caryl Rivers remembers this experience: "The bomb entered my consciousness at any early age. I remember eagerly saving box tops from KIX cereal to send away for a genuine atomic bomb. . . . The mind boggles at the notion that a weapon that killed 80,000 human beings in an afternoon could be used to hustle cereal to kids."[2]

Children in grade school, especially boys, enjoy the idea of war, with its adventure, mystery, action, and power. Thus, only if one accepts the Perrys' idea that children actually think like adults and find war unattractive, can one accept the film's premise: children are able to moralize, philosophize, and find simplistic answers concerning the causes and effects of nuclear war.

Ladybug, Ladybug, also implies that even among children only the ruthless will survive. But the children in the film, writes John Simon, "are diminutive symbols and have very little talent."[3] Though Frank Perry selected accomplished adult actors, Simon contends, "his direction is rudimentary and his wife's script is, if possible [even more difficult for] the adults."[4]

Although most of the children and adults may not have been portrayed realistically, what is significant in the film is the Perrys have effectively preserved some important attitudes of the cold war. Rivers, a child of the fifties recalls: "I remember . . . in parochial school, passing notes about the bomb back and forth to my friend Sally. We drew pictures of mushroom clouds and radioactive fish. One joke was that we didn't have to eat fish on Friday anymore, because the bomb had made them all radioactive. We didn't really worry about the bomb; we accepted it as just another of the new things that kept cropping up in our life."[5] The film's two youngest children convincingly reflect this innocent attitude. Using paper planes, they happily bomb away at imagined cities, destroying millions. They also willingly empty a glass jar filled with coins to make room for their pet frog. Rather than opting for material possessions, they prefer the frog, which is a simple reflection of humanity.

The Perrys have a limited degree of success in portraying what might happen if a civil defense alarm sounded in a rural elementary school. Not knowing whether attack was imminent, they fall into great confusion—the principal's uncertainty, the staff's hesitation, the bewildered expressions of students and teachers alike. The procedures of evacuation to places of safety via bus and by foot impart an illusion of photographed reality.[6]

Unfortunately, too often the film attempts to shock by depicting the fear of a possible nuclear explosion and the sporadic reactions of intended victims. "These are respectable intentions," writes Bosley Crowther, "but, unfortunately, the film is too slight in dramatic structure . . . the details are weakly developed and tension is barely drawn." [7] *Ladybug, Ladybug* fails to offer any suggestions on how to react to an impending nuclear attack. Additionally, the singular bit of tension and dramatic irony occurs only when it is discovered that the signal is false. "It is hardly enough," concludes Crowther, "to compensate for an audience's valuable time." [8]

9

GEORGE W. LINDEN

Dr. Strangelove Or: How I Learned to Stop Worrying and Love the Bomb

Dr. Strangelove was released in the spring of 1964. It is difficult for me to recall precisely my initial feelings and responses to this brilliant film. I do remember, however, that the audience was quite silent throughout most of the screening and that I, and others, emerged from the theater feeling subdued and heavy—as though our minds were permeated by somber pessimism. We recognized the dialogue and situations as being outrageous and hilariously funny, yet our laughter was thin and tenuous. The experience of the film was profoundly ambiguous. On reflection, I find this to be a strange reaction to a comic construction. Why did I, and other members of the audience, feel such deep ambivalence? Why did we not react to *Strangelove* as a brilliantly funny film? Why was our laughter not robust?

Three answers can be given to these questions. Each answer is based on the content, style and structure of the film itself. The first answer is in terms of the relation of *Strangelove* to our lived experience. A second answer is based on the relation of *Strangelove* to other films. A third answer is in terms of the thematic substance of *Strangelove* itself. The ultimate thesis of this article is that I, and others, originally misperceived and perhaps may still be misperceiving the thematic essence of *Dr. Strangelove*.

One reason for the ambivalent reaction of Americans to *Dr. Strangelove* was our inability to unravel the relations between the reel world and the real one. It is precisely this inability that provides much of the tension and force of the film. By use of constant crosscutting to his three basic locations and by shifting to three styles, Stanley Kubrick intensifies this tension. The plot of the film is the accelerating tech-

Dr. Strangelove Or: How I Learned to Stop Worrying and Love the Bomb.
Courtesy of Swank Motion Pictures, Inc.

nological inevitability of modern society, an acceleration that has as its products social stupidity and ultimate political impotence. Man, the real enemy, becomes subject to his infernal machines. The crazy logic of the cold war is carried to its inevitable conclusion: not merely the triggering of the atom bomb but the further superdeterrent of the diabolical doomsday machine.

Perhaps even more basic is that the film plays on our basic neurotic anxiety: total nuclear annihilation. That this anxiety is a major target of the film is shown by the rest of its title, *Or: How I Learned to Stop Worrying and Love the Bomb*. The film exploits what I would call our basal anxiety. The reasons for the intensity of this basal anxiety are many and complex. Only some of its dimensions: repression, the immediate past, and the absurdity of (what was then) present reality. Anxieties concerning these dimensions were all triggered by images, events, and styles of the film.

A brilliant director, Kubrick does not allow the resident neuroses of his audience to become neutralized. Just as the individual begins to laugh at the antics on the screen and forgets the seriousness of the plot, the director switches to another location. There are only three basic locations in the film: Burpelson Air Force Base, the bomber, and the War Room. Each shift from one location to the other is accompanied by increasing the tempo of violence. The audience is not allowed to relax and regard the movie as merely a spectacle, but instead is caught in the progressive acceleration of the film.

The increasing intensity of the mosaic of locations is accomplished by three different shifts of film styles. One style is antiseptic ironic counterpoint. This style dominates the beginning of the film, most of the scenes in the War Room, and many of the exterior shots of the bomber as it waltzes and eventually waddles to its target. The second style is brute realism. (It is this style that forces the audience to call on the real world in relation to the reel one.) The hectic excitement inside the wounded airplane is conveyed by a jerky, accelerating, hand-held camera technique. The invasion of Burpelson Air Force Base is shot in grainy newsreel texture, the camera movements are abrupt and shaky. The third style consists of cool close-ups and minimum camera movement. Here, the camera is used as a window on "reality" and the actors are allowed to carry the scenes into exaggerated absurdity. The purpose of this exaggeration was to raise the film from comedy to satire, thus neutralizing its potent appeals to fear. Unfortunately for the audience, the recent reality they were living was as absurd as the characters in the film. Thus the "neutralization" failed to take full effect. When reality itself is absurd, it is doubtful satire is possible.

General Turgidson's disbelief that the "stupid Ruskies" could shoot down his planes is absurd until we remember our own anxiety about *Sputnik*. The intense concern over a doomsday gap appears as a form of ultimate insanity until we recall the United States is pockmarked by strategic missile silos inhabited by multiple-headed hydras. Turgidson's advice to strike first and we will "get our hair mussed a bit," but we will only lose a few million people, may seem incredible until we recall a retired air force general who ran for the second highest office in the land.[1]

Another reason for the ambivalent audience reaction to *Dr. Strangelove* was the public's inability to classify the film as a comedy, a satire, or as a clever projection of reality. This raises the problem of classification and the broader problem of understanding. The puzzled reactions to the film might also be explained by the inability of the audience to recognize it as a work of its own merits. Recognition, after all, demands that we draw distinctions. Furthermore, it demands we then see the concrete work as an analogue of comparable productions. *Dr. Strangelove* did, indeed, appear strange. I have already referred to the three different styles used in the film. This complexity may have made the film hard for many to comprehend. Another reason for the difficulty of understanding, however, was the film itself displayed facets that resist the attempts to classify it as a member of a genre.

At first viewing, it seems as if *Dr. Strangelove* could be classified fairly easily in terms of its content, its plot or its theme. After all, the content concerns atomic warfare, the plot reveals the progressive enslavement of man by his own technology and the theme appears to be that modern man is his own worst enemy. Hence, one is tempted to see *Dr. Strangelove* as a comic *On The Beach*, a sardonic *Fail Safe*, or an insane *Seven Days in May*. All three of the latter films are standard studio productions which, at times, exhibit some of the best characteristics of that term. They depend on a clear-cut central plot that develops in predictable, logical sequence, and displays crisp, clear photography. All three have attractive actors under full script control doing a journeyman's job, which is adequate, and only occasionally brilliant. The films deemphasize theme and two of them use music unobtrusively to substantiate the imaged events aurally.[2] They display an uncluttered, simple, straightforward, fairly impersonal style. Any one of them could have been and may have been made by a committee. On reflection, none of these characteristics seem to apply very accurately to *Dr. Strangelove*.

The film's plot is a broken mosaic that sometimes moves logically, but sometimes (such as in the revelation of the doomsday machine) by quantum jumps. Since there are three styles interwoven throughout the three locations, the photography techniques are variable according to the expressive demands of the situation and the personal tastes of the director. The theme of *Dr. Strangelove*, though subtle, eventually dominates and determines the plot extension. Kubrick is extremely careful in his use of music and utilizes it for three different purposes. His style is intensely personal. It is a constantly shifting three-phase sonata, which could not have been done by a committee. *Dr. Strangelove* is simply not a standard Hollywood production nor even a standard studio production, such as *Lolita* or *Spartacus*. It thus signals a return to the intensely personal involvement and total control, which Kubrick attempted in his film, *The Killing*. Some evidence of the personal nature of the film is as follows: The film was shot in England because 1) Kubrick prefers to live there, 2) he received no support and, in fact, some opposition from the U.S. Air Force, 3) under these conditions he could become more totally involved in the film. He designed or approved the designs of all the technical sets, coauthored the script, directed the actors, scored the music, cut the final product, and supervised the advertising. *Dr. Strangelove* is an intensely personal film.

This almost total control of the production allows Kubrick to express three recurrent directorial dimensions, which are developed in his later films: a deemphasis on plot, an emphasis on the centrality of music, and a fascination with the future. Suffice it to say here that the theme is extended beyond the plot and ultimately determines the form of the film.[3]

The centrality of music is a dimension introduced in *Strangelove*, which later becomes obsessive in Kubrick's films. In most modern films, music is either invisible or obtrusive. In the invisible style, music allows the visuals to dominate and seldom, if ever, become a focus of attention. In such a style, the best music is the least memorable. The obtrusive, and often obtuse, use of music is best exemplified by the works of John Sturges (*The Magnificent Seven*) or Stanley Kramer (*On The Beach, Guess Who's Coming to Dinner*). Kubrick follows neither

path. He attempts, in *Dr. Strangelove*, to *weave* the aurals into the
visuals, thus creating mutual enhancement. One method of weaving is
ironic counterpoint. Another method is plot device. The third method is
subtle shifting of tonalities and a resultant shift in urgency, both aural
and visual.

The two best examples of ironic counterpoint occur at the beginning
and end of *Dr. Strangelove*. The film begins with hand-drawn titles
and a disclaimer that it refers to anyone living or dead. We then have
the sound of sweeping wind and voice-over narration concerning the
U.S. network of constant alert (primarily over the Zokoff Islands). This
is simulated realism. The camera then moves in on a B-52 nudging up
to a mother plane. As the tanker extends its long nozzle to the super-
bomber, the audio plays the old romantic, pro-feminine song, "Try a
Little Tenderness." The music modifies the visuals by adding humor,
thus making them seem less menacing, and also converts the flying into
a kind of romantic dance. At the end of the film, we have a series of
intercuts and repetitions of mushroom clouds spreading into the sky.[4]
As counterpoint to these intercuts, we have the rather fatuous Hawaiian
song, "Someday We'll Meet Again." Here, the ironic counterpoint
punches up the visuals and etches their meaning. Mushroom clouds
have been so used and reused to the point of dullness that Kubrick had
to restore some edge to his visuals.

As for weaving music as a plot device or as shifting tonality, one
should consider that when music is used as a plot device, the aurals
come to the foreground and the visuals become subordinate. This occurs
in the film when Captain Mandrake discovers the unconfiscated tran-
sistor radio at the air base. He innocently walks into General Ripper's
office and points out that if nuclear war had truly been declared, the
radio would not be blaring its normal puerile music. Ripper immediately
orders him to turn the radio off. This brings Mandrake to the horrid
realization of the actual situation, but before he can take any effective
action, Ripper confines him, thus revealing his hand (and his insanity).
As for the shifting of tonality, Kubrick uses the theme song, "When
Johnny Comes Marching Home," as an accompaniment to the one un-
controlled bomber. At first, the tune is played heavily, enhancing the
menace of the accelerating situation and visuals. Then the same tune
is carried forward by harmonica. During this sequence, the visuals are
lightened and the wounded plane almost seems to dance in tune as it
relentlessly swerves forward.[5] As the crippled bomber comes closer and

closer to its final target of opportunity, the same song reverses back to orchestral performance with muffled, accelerating drums. These subtle shifts in the aurals also determine subtle shifts in the visuals, giving the union of the two more depth and texture.

What this masterful experimentation with the visual-aural relationships suggests is that there is a category into which *Dr. Strangelove* can conveniently and meaningfully be included. At the risk of being accused of falling into auteurism, I suggest *Dr. Strangelove* can be best understood not as a comedy satire, nor as a war film, nor as an atom-bomb excursion, but as a difficult, subtle, and original Stanley Kubrick film.

If one examines the reviews of the film when it was first released, he finds the reviewers are almost unanimous in their interpretations. Some approved the film, others condemned it, but all of them agreed that the plot and theme were congruent and coextensive. Hence, they saw the plot as the difficulty of attempting to call back all the bombers and the theme as man's destruction through his subservience to his self-created technological inevitability. I must admit I also viewed the film from this vantage point. This hypothesis, however, as useful as it is, raises some problems. If the plot and theme are coextensive, then one has difficulty explaining the dominant image of the film, the title of the film, and ultimately, its structure.

While it is true that *Dr. Strangelove* ends with repeated mushroom clouds expanding behind the credits, the dominating, progressive image of the whole is that the film begins in the air and ends underground. Or, one could say it begins with an image of two superplanes in inter-course-sustenance and ends with a climax of clouds. The latter image is obviously sexual. The former image is also sexual in the extended sense of grounding. Furthermore, the dominant image is sexual in regard to its content. The airplane is being refueled so that it can jockey expectantly at its fail-safe point. It is loaded and ready to go. The last scene in the film concerns a discussion of a possible mine-shaft gap and the calculation that with ten women to every man—along with heroic endurance on the part of the men—the human race can be re-populated underground while the doomsday cloud dissipates its half-life. Either interpretation of the dominant image points to the theme as not being man's enslavement by his own technology. Though it is tempting to view the theme as Faustian, "*Am Ende hangen wir ab von Creaturen wir machten* [in the end, we are dependent on the creatures we have made]," actually the dominating image indicates that the thematic essence is an examination of some relations between Thanatos and Eros. The dominating image points to the thematic essence as erotic displacement.

With the title of the film, there exists the same difficulty. The title obviously does not express anything about technological inevitability. The subtitle, *How I Learned to Stop Worrying and Love the Bomb*, does not appear to be literal for the simple reason the audience fails to lose its uneasiness, fails to quit worrying, and does not "learn to love the bomb." One could not claim this merely reveals a failure of artistry or technique on Kubrick's part; that is, he could not embody the intention of the subtitle, or he chose the wrong title. Either of the hypotheses seems untenable, because of the superb artistry he uses in his treatment of styles, cuts, pacing camera angles, and music. As for failure of technique, the elaborate reconstruction of the mock-up B-52 might refute this claim. Since the U.S. Air Force would provide no cooperation at all on the film, Kubrick not only built a ten-foot model of a B-52 but also constructed an elaborate set for his interior shots. This set was designed on the basis of photographs he had culled from various British aviation magazines. This mock-up alone cost $100,000, and it betrays an obsession with accuracy and technological mystique, which becomes a trademark of later Kubrick films.[6]

If the subtitle is not a failure due to artistry or technique, and the audience does not learn to love the bomb, what can we conclude? We must conclude Kubrick *meant* it. We may also conclude he meant it to be meaningful, that is, symbolic. The subtitle, then, points to some perversion of love; some odd love in which one loves not the human race but bombs. The main title, after all, is not "President Muffley," "Premier Kissoff," "General Ripper" nor "General Turgidson." The main title is the name of a former Peenemunde V-2 rocket builder, Dr. Merkwuerdigichliebe, Dr. Strangelove. The significance of choosing the name of a minor, and at first thought, almost superfluous character, as the main title of the film will become apparent later. In any event, the choice of titles was no accident. This was not only one of the first films Kubrick was able to write, shoot, and edit; but it was also one of the first on which he, personally, handled the publicity. It should not be overlooked that the main title designates, denotatively, a *strange love*, a love that is somehow odd, unusual, or peculiar. The titles also point to a thematic essence of erotic displacement.

If one maintains the position of the congruence and coextensibility of the plot and theme, and if one holds the thematic substance of the film is technological inevitability gone wild, then the structure of *Dr. Strangelove* must be seen as faulty. Certainly, Robert Hatch must have viewed the film in this way for he describes the character of Dr. Strangelove as being the least persuasive and the most peripheral in the film.[7] On first viewing, I must admit I shared this view of the film. I believed the structure was too long; that the film should have ended with Kong riding down the bomb and the mushroom cloud filling the sky. The following cut to the War Room with the ensuing discussions of survival and the emergence of Dr. Strangelove himself as a dominant figure, I believed, was an unwarranted extension. Given the theme of technological inevitability, the film ought properly to have ended with the destruction of mankind. The whole last scene of the film, then, seemed to be simply an absurd anticlimax. If one sees the last scene as essential and not tangential to the film, then, one needs to reinterpret the theme. Such a reinterpretation is consistent both with the substance and structure of the film itself.

Dr. Strangelove is not merely a movie about nuclear war; it is also an attack on a basic mythic membrane: the American pornography of power. It is an attack on our propensity to substitute violence for love. That is, indeed, a strange love. In spite of our recent bloody history, we Americans still staunchly deny we are votaries of violence. A brief look at our mass media, however, will demonstrate that we are a violent people. This demonstration can be made by looking at our movies and television programs either in terms of content or censorship.

Yet it is not violence we censor. Even though some studies have shown that the repeated impact of violence, which is the constant content of our Saturday morning cartoons, does have an influence on children's behavior, that is, those bombarded become measurably more aggressive, we do not censor violence. What we do censor is nudity and sexual activity in film. No one has ever demonstrated that screen nudity is a corrupting influence. It is perfectly permissible to attack pornography or even artistic portrayals of sex. Such attacks help us to avoid facing the fact we have repressed the reality of death and embraced its mystique. Violence is as American as apple pie.[8]

Dr. Strangelove himself is desperately in love with death. But the same could be said of all the "conservatives" in the film. The true thematic essence of the film, then, is the erotic displacement that substitutes death for desire, for the mystery of the other. *Dr. Strangelove* may be one of the first modern films saying: Make Love Not War. If so, it was a herald of the new drug culture and the profound changes between the current generations of Americans. Such an hypothesis not only helps one to unify the structure of the film by making the last scene a necessary element, it also helps illuminate the survival kits issued in the fatal B-52. Besides containing weapons and food, those survival kits contained two types of things: drugs and sexual entice-ments. They contained antibiotic pills, morphine pills, vitamin pills, pep pills, sleeping pills, and tranquilizer pills. They also contained four 21-jewel Swiss watches, one hundred dollars in rubles, five gold-plated fountain pens, ten packs of chewing gum, one issue of prophylactics, three lipsticks, and three pairs of nylon stockings.

Accepting the hypothesis of erotic displacement would mean many viewers initially misperceived the film. *Dr. Strangelove* is more pro-found and prophetic than we originally took it to be.

10

MICHAEL G. WOLLSCHEIDT

Fail Safe

Recall the film experience—was it a time for asking questions, heightening awareness and sharpening perception while bursting through the banal dogmas of our time and creating art through a myriad of theme and expression? Or was that the myth? Perhaps it is impossible for the medium of film to produce something timeless in this age of instantaneous image-exchange. Although one film, one fleeting image in the history of the medium will be singled out here, the attempt will be to maintain a certain perspective. The real concern is not "one" film, but film itself.

In the middle sixties, nuclear war advanced as a topical Hollywood product. It should be asked if these films posed significant questions, provided solutions or brought new perceptions concerning the threat of nuclear war. Although there is perhaps no subject of greater importance than how a decision to use nuclear weapons might be made, there is probably no subject about which less is known. One such film examining the decision-making process, *Fail Safe*, began its journey through the media as a 1962 novel. The impact of the book was thorough; the paperback version proudly boasts the banner "Over Two Million Copies Sold." The story provided exciting reading for a public caught in an avalanche of ominous warnings of a mushroom cloud looming on the horizon. The authors, Eugene Burdick and Harvey Wheeler, composed an exciting story, yet one expects their enthusiasm came from effectively reading the public. They could rely on success—nuclear warfare was an exploitable topic.

But *Fail Safe* encountered difficulties even before it reached a film producer's hands. Another novel and film concerning nuclear war be-

Fail Safe. Courtesy of Twyman Films, Inc.

came strangely intertwined in the *Fail Safe* story. *Fail Safe* attracted much attention when it was initially published, particularly from the author of a 1958 novel entitled *Red Alert*. The two stories were remarkably similar, and a suit for plagiarism ensued.[1] No doubt, to the relief of Burdick and Wheeler, the case was finally settled out of court. Interestingly, *Red Alert* returned to haunt *Fail Safe*—albeit changed in form and title—as Stanley Kubrick employed it as the basis for his brilliant and darkly humorous film, *Dr. Strangelove*.[2] This interesting parallel continued—both films were released in the same year—1964. (*Dr. Strangelove* premiered in New York in January, *Fail Safe*, in September.) Although political rhetoric was dominant at the time, the nuclear scare was waning. No longer distributed were civil defense pamphlets, which mapped escapeways from congested cities and charted anticipated numbers of casualties in neat, regimented tables of percentages. Man had survived, the race to oblivion seemed to have temporarily yielded. Two films were plunged into this curious cauldron of emotion with quite interesting results. It proved most unfortunate for the producers of *Fail Safe*, when Kubrick's *Dr. Strangelove* came out first. When *Fail Safe* appeared in print, it was a fairly accurate reflection of our growing concern about the nuclear threat. By 1964, however, society was much more attuned to the black humor of *Dr. Strangelove*, while *Fail Safe* tried to be serious *after* we had passed the point of all-consuming concern. The key to the effectiveness of *Fail Safe* or any film of its genre is one's perception of the seriousness of man's condition in relation to nuclear war. Perhaps this perception is reflected in most productions concerning the bomb. The final holocaust is almost always triggered by an electromechanical malfunction. In fact, if any human miscalculation is involved, it is of the moment and almost totally unrelated to the fact that such weapons exist.

Nevertheless, one must either accept or reject the story's premise: An accident similar to the one depicted in *Fail Safe* is mathematically inevitable. But it seems that many did not believe this film when it was released. Reviews of *Fail Safe*, describing it as a "science-fantasy," suggest the implausibility of the story. A brief historical review of the film should provide some insight into the film's limited effectiveness.

Fail Safe contends the only solution to a mechanical malfunction is the immolation of innocents. The malfunction at the Omaha headquarters of the Strategic Air Command sends bombers streaking past their fail safe points on a heading for Moscow. Their mission is to destroy the Soviet capital with nuclear bombs. The president of the United States rushes to the hotline to inform the Soviet premier that not only are the planes beyond recall, but it is all a terrible accident. Two wrongs seem to make a right in international power politics. To prove the whole affair is an innocent mistake, the president (Henry Fonda), is forced to swap New York for Moscow, to trade one annihilated city for another.

In the final scene, the screen resembles a painter's canvas or a still photograph. Director Sidney Lumet combines the zoom with the freeze-frame, creating a dramatic rhythm within the shot. The zoom-freeze selects significant details. As one bomber approaches New York, for example, Lumet cuts from the plane to shots showing New Yorkers at work and play—a woman hanging out wash, an irate taxi driver, children happily roller skating, and birds in flight. Their behavior reflects the motions of life and normalcy. Then the bomb falls. Lumet uses a collection of stills from this sequence: he employs the zoom-freeze on each of the several figures of the previously shown stills, implying that the New Yorkers die in a single instant.[3]

The story effectively weaves a fictional version of what is at stake as a global community. The growing tension gives rise to a feeling of personal involvement. Dramatic scenes of the president facing the inevitable decision, the grotesque hotline phone looming on his desk, and the placid looks of his interpreter in an otherwise barren room, all emphasize the loneliness he must feel. That phone and the interpreter are all that remain of his nation's "security."

Most of the action in *Fail Safe* takes place in only three settings, the Pentagon's War Conference Room, an underground room in the White House and Strategic Air Command (SAC) headquarters in Omaha. Director Sidney Lumet maximizes suspense and emotional tension by permitting his cast to behave as intelligent men faced with an impending catastrophe. As the president, Henry Fonda soberly and emphatically instructs his Russian interpreter (Larry Hagman) to analyze not only the Soviet premier's words, but his thoughts: "I want to know . . . what you think he's feeling; it's important that we understand each other."

Unable to recall the American bombers or to shoot them all down with American fighter planes, Fonda instructs the SAC general (Frank Overton) to inform the Soviet Union of their location. Intent on con-

vincing the Russians it was a mistake, the general makes available all
necessary data—the Russians, with SAC's assistance, attempt to shoot
down the bombers. In Omaha, the location and fate of the bombers is
kept under surveillance by a large electronic plotting map. Grady
(Edward Binns), the pilot of the single bomber to reach Moscow, refuses to adhere to appeals from the President and his own wife. Following set orders, he releases the megaton bombs which, in turn, forces
Fonda to destroy New York City.

In *Fail Safe*, the President and the Soviet premier discuss the helplessness of their respective situations while waiting for Moscow to be
razed by American bombers. The theme of their soul-searching conversation is that no one is to blame. The decisions regarding nuclear weapons are almost of a mystical nature, beyond capacity to comprehend or
control. The president, for example, prior to the dropping of four
20-megaton bombs over Moscow and New York, explains the forth-
coming holocaust to the Russian premier—

> This crisis of ours—this accident as you say. . . . In one way it's no
> man's fault. No human being made any mistake, and there's no point in
> trying to place the blame on anyone. . . . This disappearance of human
> responsibility is one of the most disturbing aspects of the whole thing. It's
> as if human beings had evaporated, and their places were taken by com-
> puters. And all day you and I have sat here, fighting, not each other, but
> rather the big rebellious computerized system, struggling to keep it from
> blowing up the world.

Responds the Russian premier: "It is true, Mr. President. Today the
whole world could have been burned without any man being given a
chance to have a say in it."[4]

Films about the bomb have consistently stressed that the action of the
United States government in dropping atomic bombs on Japan quite
probably sealed the fate of atomic energy for years thereafter. From
1945 onward, the potential of a great and historic scientific discovery
was doomed to the perversion of mass annihilation. Atomic energy,
baptized in war, grew from an enfant terrible to a thermonuclear tyrant.
One must, along with the rational leaders of our time, coexist with the
threat.

The historical record reveals that the unrivaled terror of Hiroshima
and Nagasaki momentarily stunned governmental, scientific, and even
military leaders into a serious reconsideration of the value of the atomic
bomb and its inevitable progeny. Men of diverse background and ex-

perience, such as Albert Einstein and General Douglas MacArthur, made public their doubts and pleaded for increased awareness of the danger and waste of nuclear arms. Along with his plea for international control of atomic energy, Einstein expressed awareness of the difficulties in gaining acceptance for such proposals. In *Out of My Later Years* Einstein wrote, with a sense of cautious optimism, that he was confident such a course would eventually be recognized as the most economically feasible solution.[5] It is significant that men as diverse as these—-Einstein, a proclaimed pacifist, and MacArthur, a proven warrior—both perceived the folly of a frenzied arms race.

Furthermore, sentiments of this nature did receive recognition in the critical years following World War II. Some study was devoted to the possibility of international control of atomic energy, specifically halting the development of dangerous weapon systems by individual nations. Naturally, the development of peaceful uses of atomic energy would have remained completely open and unrestricted.[6] Research makes it apparent that during this period numbers of people remained unconvinced that atomic energy should have continued as a charge for the ultimate cannon of doom. These apprehensions were strongly prevalent in the middle sixties.

Yet why have most films apparently failed to sharpen one's knowledge of nuclear war? Perhaps understanding the nuclear threat, as depicted on film, is necessarily determined by the perception of the medium itself. At present, film is perhaps the only art form that communicates ideas to a mass audience, but it is not widely understood as a major contributor to the communication process. Similarly, film as primarily an esthetic experience seems terribly avant-garde. We appear to have enlisted the aid of this new invention, art form, and industry in our attempt to escape reality and enter the long-sought refuge of private fantasy.

Fail Safe questions preventive nuclear war. In theory, an intimidated nation might force a world leader into using his awesome power to undermine an imagined threat—striking first in a defensive sense. But such a "preventive" maneuver would be a travesty in every sense; that nation could be initiating a worldwide holocaust. Such a philosophy makes use of Orwellian logic: The bomb is our deliverance; salvation will come through destruction. In the end, the irony of our nuclear "security" is the paranoia it creates.

This fear and panic is exemplified in *Fail Safe* by the fanatic scientist who advises the president to make the most of a hopeless situation—he asks the president to destroy the Communist threat forever with a total first strike. But in this film the situation has been given added meaning. A terrified nation has not forced the president's hand; the first stroke was a mistake and cannot be halted. Thus, a preventive war becomes a war not to destroy the enemy but to placate him. Waging war on itself, the United States must forsake New York City to prevent a global fireball.

But for all the cinematic horror and suspense of the freeze-frame death of New York City, the film fails because it leaves one feeling more uneasy than truly fearful, more sorrowful than indignant. While portraying the world's precarious position, *Fail Safe* only furthers the myth and cruel hypocrisy of our nuclear age. The underlying theme of the story is that man was long ago overwhelmed by events; nuclear energy was preordained to become an all-powerful demon. Therefore, no blame may be affixed for man was impotent in the face of an irresistible force. Yet history illustrates warnings were sounded.

Fail Safe does not offer any hope that as a nation, and ultimately as a global community, we will acknowledge our responsibility for the present condition of man. Who is responsible is not so important as the fact that responsibility should indeed be assigned to someone. In the final analysis, man is the victim of imagined senses of impotence and innocence.

Hollywood films about nuclear war seem to have failed in casting man in the starring role. Responsibility is placed elsewhere and, as a result, the audience is not insulted or challenged. *Fail Safe*, in accordance with the consumer psychology, dares only to present us with a reflection of what we have imagined about recent history, the present condition of the world, and our influence on both.

In recalling the film experience, we have discovered a community of artists armed with the strategies of business. Their films are designed, as all products must be, to exist for a specific time, audience, and price: an evening at the movies with your friend and mine—the bomb. As a consequence, film has come to reflect what we are—consumers.

We need not be satisfied with film as a mirror image, for its very essence is a dual nature of capacity and purpose. Film could surpass other art forms in the capacity to communicate ideas on a mass scale and eclipse the other mass media in the purposeful adherence to artistic principles. In its treatment of nuclear war, film could truly gain prominence as a communicative art form by transcending the mirror image of the blinding fail safe flash and passing bravely through the looking glass to the desolate reality beyond.

Fail Safe, despite its simplistic theme—the overreliance on mechanical efficiency—effectively presents the dilemma of man threatened with destruction by his own technology. Director Lumet achieves strong, positive performances from his cast. The film is tautly constructed and although not quite as significant as other nuclear war films, it remains, nonetheless, an important and meaningful motion picture.

11

KAMIL WINTER

The Bedford Incident

What is there that could still be remarkable in a Hollywood motion picture, whose story was labeled weak, whose direction was at best average, and whose performance of its otherwise well-established actors (Richard Widmark, Sidney Poitier and Martin Balsam) was not quite up to expectations? It seemed clear that *The Bedford Incident* could not have survived as excellent entertainment. In the context of nuclear war films, however, *The Bedford Incident* has its place, and a unique one at that.

Like any work of art, it is, with or without the intention of its creators, a product of its environment and thus reflects the values and ideas of society at that time. At first glance, the film does this by virtue of its central theme—the threat of nuclear conflagration. Different from most nuclear war films, however, it does not aim to depict the full reality of nuclear war such as the documentary, *Hiroshima-Nagasaki—August, 1945*—a reality that has already become almost obsolete in view of the thirty more years of scientific progress. Nor does it claim membership in the science-fiction club which offered *The Day the Earth Caught Fire*, or in the simulated cinéma vérité style represented by *The War Game*. For better or for worse, *The Bedford Incident* is simply entertainment. Its story, weak or not, does not concentrate on the bomb, its potential or its effect, but on human relations, on human profiles, and on the not-so-classical environment of nuclear warships in the nuclear age. Therein lies its unique quality and relevance.

Viewing *The Bedford Incident* today, one feels relieved by the manner in which many of the prevailing or even dominant features of those times have lost their urgency, become outdated, and almost unreal. The cold war atmosphere, without which the emergence of films such as *The Bedford Incident* would be unthinkable, has been replaced by a spirit of détente and conciliation. The belief in the probability, if not inevitability, of armed conflict between the superpowers has given way to the universally pronounced expression of hope that such a conflict would be tragic, unnecessary, and irrational. In short, only one of the main aspects of the background from which *The Bedford Incident* emerged seems to have survived to this day—the existence of the bomb.

This reality is likely to survive many other possible changes yet to appear on the international political scene. The bomb is here, and mankind is forced to coexist with it. It would be naïve to assume the nuclear monster will either disappear by itself or be made to do so by some imaginary, concerted human effort. No invention of science has as yet been intentionally destroyed by man because it contained potential destruction. Therefore, the easy solution—Destroy the Bomb!—is not a solution. In the final analysis, it is *not* the existence of the bomb itself but man's use of the bomb and the relations between men that pose the problem. It still is man's finger that triggers final, total destruction.

This problem has become increasingly complex in view of the inherent dehumanizing factor of nuclear weapons. Historians have noted that in the past adversaries came face-to-face with each other, measured and tested each other as individual human beings, developing the ultimate human effort to kill—a release of individual human emotion. With the invention of gunpowder and the progressing mechanization of its means of delivery, not only did it become technically simpler to kill, it also became humanly easier because, with increasing distance, the face of the enemy appeared blurred and its expressions unrecognizable. Today's age of sophisticated missiles, tanks, bomber-spy planes, and underground Pentagons has eliminated the individual—modern weaponry and human beings have now become a single anonymous entity. The nuclear bomb, carried by intercontinental rockets, has erased the last trace of human contact between the killer and his victim. Total destruction is joined by total dehumanization. Perhaps it is no coincidence that in his first thirty years of coexistence with the bomb, man has been preoccupied with the former while almost ignoring the latter.

Most films on nuclear war concentrate on mechanical effects—the terrible destructive power of the bomb. They support the view that nuclear war is terrible and irrational because it is so destructive—there will be no victor and no vanquished. Characteristically, the numbers game has been played by both the opponents as well as advocates of nuclear madness. The opponents find no one shall be alive following the nuclear holocaust; the advocates try to prove scientifically that sufficient numbers shall survive to perpetuate postnuclear life.

The Bedford Incident does not show us the results of the destructive power of the nuclear bomb. Instead, it depicts the drama of men in close confinement, the relentless pursuit of military superiority during the cold war. An intransigent captain (Richard Widmark) of an American destroyer on patrol in North Atlantic waters, an element of the North Atlantic Treaty Organization, has an obsessive determination to hunt a Soviet submarine. Widmark continually forces his crew to monitor and then close in on the Russian warship whenever feasible. He refuses to follow the advice of his fellow officers who warn him against taking inordinate risks; the ship's medical officer (Martin Balsam) and the NATO attaché from West Germany (Eric Portman) also fail to convince him to refrain from tracking the submarine. Widmark, however, maintains his tragic maneuvering until the fatal accident occurs.

Although he is not seen on camera, the Russian commander is obviously equally adamant; he resists all attempts of harassment and challenges the American destroyer. The unyielding pressures serve only to strengthen his purpose and the relentless chase resumes among floating ice fields off the Greenland coast. Both he and Widmark represent great forces of power; they are arrogant, shrewd, energetic, and not easily swayed. Although their intellectual and physical abilities are balanced, each man believes he is superior; there is no subsequent compromise. Their tenacity and innate fixedness of purpose shows, in a compelling manner, the terrifying atmosphere of dehumanization that is caused by the floating IBM.

In spite of James B. Harris's taut, skillful direction, however, the film transcends plausibility; as a reporter, for example, Sidney Poitier has complete run of the ship; he is even permitted to take photographs of this sensitive mission. As the ensign who releases the fatal antisub rockets, James MacArthur is impressive, but his firing mistake is too obvious, lacking conviction.

The Bedford Incident effectively illustrates how, amidst this labyrinth of perfected automation, the one instinct inherited from man's animalistic predecessors paves the way and ultimately leads to the incidental catastrophic climax—the hunter's instinct. This pernicious obsession with the hunt transcends the frontiers of patriotic and soldierly duty, obscuring the fine basic human qualities which thousands of years of civilization have implanted in the human heart and mind.

Some criticisms reveal a lack of logic in the film. They question the believability of the captain and his floating IBM, which hunts its Russian equivalent with the obsession of a prehistoric monster. Can the captain logically disregard any other feeling and dictate of reason? The clash between the ultimate achievement of human reason and this animalistic relic in human nature is illogical. It justifies the implication that this inconsistent conflict makes sense. How many other equally glaring, pointed contradictions or psychologisms can be found in our world? Does it not seem illogical that scientific and technological progress has provided a hitherto unheard-of abundance, and yet, hundreds of millions of human beings still cannot satisfy their basic human needs?

Science and technology have enabled man to cross continents in a matter of hours, yet human beings living only a few scores of miles apart remain unable to communicate with one another. Science and technology have created the capacity for us to leave our atmosphere and explore strange planets, yet we are threatened with death by breathing the poisoned air on our own.

These and other contradictions exist in our world. Humanity has discovered the most mysterious laws of its environment, yet it remains unable to come to grips with itself. The most sophisticated computers, the most powerful nuclear devices will be unable to close this gap. *The Bedford Incident* serves to assist us in becoming aware of four significant questions: 1) How can we prevent our whole planet from being converted into a floating IBM, reassert human values, establish new interhuman relationships compatible with the achievements and results of scientific and technological developments? 2) How valid is the code of human behavior, for individuals as well as for societies, which includes such values as duty, honor, patriotism, and many more, established and handed down to us from the time of the sword? 3) How valid is it today in the age of the bomb? And is it indeed appropriate, even thinkable, to accept violence, any violence, as a means to establish relations between men? 4) Shall we reconcile ourselves to the fact that basically we are to remain a species dividing itself into hunters and hunted?

Alert observers may detect that behind the façade of conventional and perhaps not even superb entertainment, *The Bedford Incident* does point in the direction of these highly relevant questions and it does raise, or at least hint at, such queries. If, being a product destined for mass consumption, this film has helped to increase the number of those who are becoming aware of the complexities as well as the urgency of the problem, namely the very existence of mankind in the nuclear age, it deserves credit for fulfilling an important social function.

2
DOCUMENTARIES AND EDUCATIONAL SHORT FILMS

12

JACK G. SHAHEEN

A Thousand Cranes:
Children of Hiroshima

The atomic destruction of Hiroshima, as presented in Betty
Jean Lifton's film, *A Thousand Cranes: Children of Hiroshima*, offers
touching moments of realism. The purpose as stated in the sensitive
film is, "To inform American children about what it is like to be a child
in Hiroshima . . . to make a plea for peace." In spite of its noble
intent, the film unfortunately lacks the technical expertise and com-
petency of production characterized in other nuclear genre documentaries. The film is intensely personal, as opposed to the slick,
impersonal professionalism of other network-produced or government-
sponsored efforts. Although there are some lapses in continuity and
production, the meaning and significance of the film remains intact.
Cranes, which was written, narrated, produced, directed, and edited
by Lifton, contains a strongly individual character, causing the viewer
to feel he is in one-to-one communication with the film maker. The
central message is not overcome by the sometimes unprofessional and
choppy editing. At times, cinematic structure wavers; the narration becomes out of synchronization with screen action; and indoor sequences
are overexposed due to ineffective flood lighting. What might also be
disturbing to some viewers with opposing viewpoints is the film's
consistently overbearing, lofty moral tone.

A crane, notes Lifton, "could live a thousand years; fold a thousand
cranes and they will protect you from illness." She explains that the
protected crane comes from an old Japanese folk saying, and when the
city of Hiroshima lay in ruins, sympathizers from all over the country
began sending folded paper cranes to relatives, friends, and strangers

in the hospitals. The legend asks acceptance that the power of a thousand cranes could match the power of one atomic bomb.[1]

When Lifton went to Hiroshima in 1962 to produce *Cranes*, she had a budget of one thousand dollars. With such limited funds, the quality could not be professional, yet she felt it was more important to get her subject on film rather than be held back by inadequate financing. On returning to New Haven, Connecticut, she began editing on weekends, using a film splicer at a local camera shop. Following the editing, she wrote the narration to match selected scenes. She then recorded her own dialogue at a friend's studio in New York. (This procedure probably accounts for the overlapping narration that occasionally fails to match the visuals.) Lifton hoped *Cranes* would "say something to the hearts of men and women on this planet Earth—before it is too late. That it would help them understand that Hiroshima is not just the past, but the all-too-possible future."[2]

An advocacy film, *Cranes* seeks to effect change. Those agreeing with its message should experience a heightened sense of concern. Those who disagree will most probably dismiss its dovish theme as being naïve and idealistic. At times, the film appears too self-conscious and self-indulgent; the information is too obvious and trite. Even so, Lifton's personal approach generally shows restraint in treatment of the subject matter. She has carefully organized a collection of data and given it meaningful structure and form, albeit highly emotional in content.

Cranes reveals that today, in Hiroshima, the bomb continues to claim new victims. It gives some examination to the psychological and physical wounds of survivors of the bomb. The often harsh conditions of life after exposure to the explosion and its atomic radiation are interfaced (in an odd contradiction) against the subdued, gentle, and sometimes immature presentation and tone of the film. It creates a quiet, understated mood enhanced by David Jahn's gentle Japanese music (a delicate mosaic of flute tones), Akinori Fujii's rhythmic photography, and Lifton's soft-spoken narration. Her direction interposes sensitive philosophic meanings on which horrible facts, defying comprehension, are revealed. First, a father must undergo daily transfusions. Second, a young, attractive teacher can never wed, for no one will marry a bomb survivor (*hibakusha*, as they are called, the "explosion-affected people"). The teacher must instead transfer her affection to her students, for she will never give birth to her own baby. Survivors of Hiroshima may have genetic damage—deformities, anemia, jaundice, leukemia, and cancer. Without warning, children suddenly become orphaned or die. Radiation-weakened families are rushed to hospitals where their remaining years are spent waiting for death. Victims incapacitated by the bomb perform whatever tasks are possible.

Cranes' poetic intensity focuses on the plight of bomb survivors by introducing the memory of the Anne Frank of Hiroshima, Sodako Sasaki, a girl who died ten years after the fateful August day in 1945; she was only two years of age when the bomb fell. Sodako died, having folded only 964 of her thousand paper cranes. Her epitaph, "Paper Crane, I shall write 'peace' on your wing and you shall fly all over the world." Softly urging that we should heed her message, the film effectively illustrates what atomic bombs do to survivors in search of family, to children who watched shattered window glass lacerate their mothers and fathers, to the people of Hiroshima who observed a city literally explode and vanish.

To convey this thesis, Lifton does not show the bomb or its aftermath. Instead, we witness the inscription at the base of the Children's Monument in Hiroshima's Peace Park, "This is our cry, this is our prayer: peace in the world." We are offered insight into the Folded Crane Club, its radiation-affected founders and location in a ramshackle lean-to behind the Atomic Dome, the A-bomb hospital, an "atomic photograph" (the image of a man trying to find a shelter, etched by the bomb's bright flash into the stone façade of a bank building), an island boy's camp (originally constructed to provide for orphaned bomb survivors), and Sodako's monument. The children of the city and their families are seen behaving in a routine manner, waiting for the time when the bomb's strange, mysterious and often unpredictable effects may take their toll on life.

The Lifton film reminds us that each year on August 6 the Children of the Cranes place thousands of paper boats carrying lighted candles afloat in the river. Seeking to keep the memory alive, each lantern bears the name of a child victim. Despite its lack of professionalism and obvious technical problems, *A Thousand Cranes: Children of Hiroshima* is a successful film; it reaches out with a pertinent message of pain and love, presenting a poetic dramatization of a child's suffering as manifest in Hiroshima. Lifton's tone may at times be maudlin, but empathy on the part of the viewer is the general (and elicited) result.

13 WILLIAM MEYER

War in Short

In the early 1960s, technology seemed to have outraced the politics of arms control. Growing East-West missile buildups, development of tactical nuclear weapons suitable for limited wars, France's entry into the arms race, increased United States and Russian aboveground testing, early stalemated disarmament talks at Geneva, and neighborhood bomb shelters all dramatized the danger of thermonuclear war. The anxieties of the period brought forth a new wave of short films with a clearly defined social purpose. The film makers offered a new awareness in the context of possible nuclear warfare.

Short films can be especially effective educational vehicles. They may exercise a given theme, such as atomic war, fully in a confined space; the narration and imagery of the anguish of war and its devastation can avoid the intolerable repetition of some of the longer feature films. If it has any characterization, it can turn the nuclear film genre's usual grotesqueries, caricatures, and stereotypes into useful short-term functionaries. I have selected four atomic shorts that should be seen for their educational messages as well as their artistry.

The four—*H-Bomb over U.S.* (1962), *23 Skidoo* (1964), *A Short Vision* (1956) and *The Hole* (1962)—might well be shown to film classes in a series illustrating a wide range of cinematic techniques and styles. They should be examined in some detail to determine to what extent they are coherent and evocative as propaganda statements or as fictionalized film art. These films are not opaque, but their very brevity and the dominance of their messages could easily allow the viewer to overlook their structured significance.

The Hole. Courtesy of John Hubley

Of the four, *H-Bomb over U.S.* is the most direct propaganda. It is based on an investigation made by the Center for the Study of Democratic Institutions, which was published under the title *Community of Fear*. Its appeal is primarily rational, but its visual embellishments are decidedly emotional. The film shows the devastation that would result if a 10-megaton hydrogen bomb were dropped on the city of Los Angeles (the nuclear firepower available in 1962 was equal to ten tons of TNT for every inhabitant of the earth). *H-Bomb* also notes that bombs could be delivered by missiles in less than thirty minutes from Moscow to the United States; the estimated destruction was considered to be over five thousand miles covered by lethal levels of radiation. These are all vividly rendered by the use of animation, maps, charts, miniatures, and live action.

The narrator's calm voice tells us to forget the cities, they would be rubble, and consider the difficulties of survival in the countryside. He asks, "Will anyone want to survive?" The answer is self-evident from what the director, George Zabriskie, has shown us. Interspersed throughout, Zabriskie focuses on human hands at work, play, and prayer. The penultimate shot is of a skeleton. The final scene is of the United Nations building and the biblical text on its walls: "They shall beat their swords into plowshares." (An almost identical shot was used three years earlier in MGM's, *The World, the Flesh, and the Devil*.) Zabriskie's *H-Bomb over U.S.* remains an effective educational film that visualizes and humanizes the statistics of nuclear holocaust.

Julian Biggs's *23 Skidoo* is a fictional treatment of the postblast scene. Without narration or dialogue, Biggs employs varied auditory and visual images paced in his eight minutes of film for multiple building climaxes. His images are skillfully juxtaposed and overlapped, and a sense of what was, and what is now lost, is heightened by the interplay of shadow and light. Linear progression horizontals, verticals, and circles—also serve to formulate meaning. The ear and the eye follow Biggs on a quick trip from speeding train to circularly blowing scraps of paper and the final whiteout.

The scenes are eerie and desolate. After moving horizontally with the rapid train to city streets, the camera pans up vertical canyons of grayness, up a darkened escalator to the light of a deserted arcade, where it cuts away to black rows of crops and then to railroad tracks leading off into infinity. Down a hallway it rushes through a Kafkaesque office with rows and rows of empty desks. Suddenly, the camera cuts back to one desk, as if to say, "what's that?"

To the accompaniment of loud and distorted melodramatic violins, we learn from a teletype machine that the neutron bomb was hailed as "the greatest military breakthrough." Sound and sight coalesce again when the roar of the absent crowd at the baseball field is accentuated by lines of empty benches. At the playground, we hear children's voices and follow an invisible child down the soft curve of a slide and then on to swings whose shadows resemble machines of torture or hanging ropes blowing in the breeze. Biggs cuts to a shadow of a child's toy phantom jet cast on one of two white, head-impressioned bedroom pillows. The final shot, pieces of newspaper swirling to macabre music, suggest the total futility of man's printed words to bring the world to reason together.

In the film *23 Skidoo*, everything is intact, except there are no human beings. This type of postblast world for the survivors could be more terrible than the wasteland of thermonuclear war. Since the film's sense of finality would preclude mass escape, one might assume the literal possibility that there are no corpses because this area is on the fringe of the blast. The film is a photographic essay depicting a terrifying vision of total annihilation; unique visuals of disintegration heighten the impact, communicating a mood designed to stimulate discussion about the relative value of human life.

Joan and Peter Foldes populate their film *A Short Vision* with human and animal life; their method is to employ stills, paintings, drawings, and animations that show imaginatively the bomb's effects.

Of the soaring black object seen outside the narrator's window, he says, "I saw it approach through the deep blind sky . . . because it was so powerful it moved swiftly, noiselessly, irresistibly. It came unnoticed and uninvited." The object takes on multiple shapes. Its mystery lies in its shape shifting between animate and inanimate forms. Momentarily, at least, it resembles hundreds of sighted and sketched UFOs, which are always conceived on principles of terrestrial engineering. But the initial focus of *A Short Vision* is on the object as threat, perhaps all the more horrible because it soars so gracefully and has been loosed so inexplicably. The narrator declares, "The people were asleep when it flew over the city, but their leaders looked up and their wise men looked up . . . but it was too late."

The animals below, existing in an exotic Henri Rousseau-like natural state, sense it as alien and flee. The narrator explains, "When it flew over the mountains, the leopard looked up and the deer darted free of the tearing claws . . . and they both hid in fear."

These animals prey upon each other but theirs is a natural state, usually interrupted only by the engines of man's bad judgment. The animals symbolize innocence—and prey and predator alike are victims. The human population, too, allies and enemies, leaders and led, perish. The narrator intones, "Mountains, fields, cities and the earth will also disappear."

The monologue with its biblical syntax and language contributes a sense of moral seriousness. But another element in the film, its handling of what one might call "art as reality," seems to be what is most original and effective.

Instead of witnessing the destruction of the Basque town of Guernica, it is as though we were seeing the destruction of Picasso's painting. The arrangement of images in the film is from the shape-shifting black flying object, to the stylized animals, to the nearly representational human forms. The sense of loss is intensified by the distortion of images themselves and by their giving way to further configurations sans man. Overlaying the myth of innocence is the idea that man's best creation, his art objects, are erased by his hand; man is witnessed as the destroyer of all things.

In the end, the flying black object reappears as a moth attracted instinctively to a playful, almost human, dancing flame. The moth dips and swoops and finally perishes in the fire, which then flickers out. One of nature's least is consumed by the tiny flame, the fire which for humankind can create or destroy. The black flying object of the beginning has become a blackened screen reminding us that man's fellow creatures and his best creations might pass prematurely from this earth.

John and Faith Hubley's *The Hole* portrays the subject of thermonuclear war in a much lighter vein than the previous three films. This adult animated cartoon exploits one's preconditioned, fatuous response to the genre. It invites us to laugh along with the two comically drawn figures, one black and one white, who are underground in a New York street excavation. They work a little but mostly they chop logic on causality and chance. Underneath the surface wit and pleasantry, the Hubleys want us to see what could happen, what does happen, with or without human intervention. A giant weight may accidentally topple from a crane, but the two men will survive as do Donald Duck and Mickey Mouse in Walt Disney's animated crises. In the final shot of the charred landscape, however, we see, as in the minds of the two men, the horror that will not be transformed with the next frame. The two street workers (voices of Dizzy Gillespie and George Mathews) are opposed in their views. Understanding human error, the black man knows all about the best laid plans of men. His argument, however, comes to finding causes everywhere. The white worker, on the other hand, believes "99 percent of the people in accidents want to get hurt." Yet he shows by his actions the vagaries of chance. *The Hole* suggests cause and circumstance may both be operating to bring about ill effects or that even when we know a cause, we don't prevent the effects. Plates are broken, people are hit crossing the street, disarmament agreements are breached, and a button may be pushed releasing ICBMs.

While the dialogue occurs, a tiny, determined, buck-toothed mole burrows into the earth. The mole accidentally sets into action a radar monitor and a bespangled, five-star general. The toylike missiles, however, are shut up again in their neat little boxes when the happy-but-embarrassed mole pops up through the floor of the control room. This time the missiles are not unleashed, but the heavy weight suspended over the hole does slide from its container and fall into the excavation. The crane operator, the radar monitor, Charlie the bucket lowerer, the general, and the mole certainly do not want to cause catastrophe, yet each nearly does so.

At appropriate moments, the camera cuts away from the cartoon hole to scenes of swimming nightmarish cobalt blues, rust browns, and gore reds that characterize offensive and defensive military paraphernalia. In the end, the two workers stare wide-eyed, scared and scarred within from the near miss of the heavy weight. We know they see the conclusion of the prefaced, foreshadowing missile stockpiles. Dizzy Gillespie's voice fades in with, "Now that you've gone and left me, I'm settin' on top of this world." Discussion is over; they were lucky to survive. The little mole remains, obliviously digging his holes. Weak-eyed, capable only of distinguishing light from dark, he burrows on, seeking food, warmth, and nests. Like him, we can make mountains of rubble from the molehills of myopic indifference.

Each of the previously discussed films reveals more information with closer viewing. *H-Bomb over U.S.* suggests contemporary social issues can be developed with minimal funds. *23 Skidoo* is nearly a visual cliché in the last quarter of the twentieth century, but film students may learn much from its integral pacing and tight structure. *A Short Vision* and *The Hole* transcend their antiwar themes. They are fresh and timeless and should remain so even when the threat of nuclear war is a chapter in distant history.

14

The Decision to Drop
the Bomb

In May of 1955 Americans were able to witness a special televised event—the Yucca Flat 35-kiloton A-bomb test. A Survival City, complete with clothing store dummies called the "darlings," was erected under the joint sponsorship of CBS and NBC. The networks' purpose was to show the effects of an A-bomb on such items as the darlings' baby food, dishwashers, and children's nightgowns.[1]

The 1955 blast was postponed for nine days, because of inclement weather; when it did occur, the networks' initial enthusiasm had begun to waver. Eminent network journalists who first intended to "personalize the bomb" from trenches only thirty-five thousand yards away, were in New York at the time of detonation. A film of the Yucca Flat explosion was shown on the *Home* show, but only for a brief five minutes—before a lesson on meringue whipping.[2]

By 1965, however, public opinion had changed; people had been shaken by the cold war. As a result, television's nuclear image had matured. On 5 January 1965, the National Broadcasting Company telecast Fred Freed's *The Decision to Drop the Bomb*, a ninety-minute documentary depicting the events that began on 12 April 1945 and concluded when the decision to drop the atomic bomb on Hiroshima became reality on 6 August 1945.

The *Decision* is not concerned with the moral issue of whether the bomb should have been dropped but rather with the relationship of the events leading to the final decision. It makes no direct accusations against those scientists who developed the bomb, and no emotional comments are made on the victims. Fred Freed concentrates on illustrating how complex decisions are made by the government. As a journalist-historian, he reconstructs a rationale for men's actions. He contends there were many factors leading to the decision: the reluctance of the Japanese to surrender, the Russian demand for postwar concessions, the defeat of Germany, and the two-billion-dollar appropriation to develop atomic bombs.[3] Many events seemed unrelated at the time, yet, as Freed illustrates, they were all contributing factors in the decision to drop the bomb.

History records the day of President Harry S Truman's decision as July 25. General Leslie R. Groves, the military man who directed the Manhattan Project, contends the decision was implicit when Roosevelt ordered the bomb to be built in 1944, and was only endorsed by those who came after him. The film never suggests Groves's theory, nor does it make an issue over the warning Japan was to receive before the bombing. Fred Freed and Len Giovanitti, in their book, *The Decision to Drop the Bomb*, note the directive to bomb Japan was activated twenty-four hours before the surrender warning was given.[4] This was no longer a political question but a military operation, and the military mission was to release atomic bombs over Japan as soon as possible.

Concerning the question of whether a demonstration should be arranged for Japanese officials, Secretary of State James F. Byrnes gave one important reason—the fear that American prisoners of war might have been forced into the demonstration area. Assistant Secretary of War John L. McClory drew up an ultimatum for Japan warning the emperor of America's military effectiveness and demanding unconditional surrender.[5] An immediate surrender would spare Japan further destruction and maintain the governing authority of the imperial regime. The Japanese cabinet responded to McClory's ultimatum by issuing a statement which contained the Japanese word *mokusatsu*. *Mokusatsu* has several meanings, two of which are "ignores" and "has no comment at this time." The former was the American translation. Had the latter phrase been used—and that may have been the intended meaning—the atomic bombs might never have been released over Japan. Unfortunately, although many Japanese wanted to end the war there were strong rival factions. Prime Minister Suzuki Kantarō attempted to have the Russians mediate, thus keeping the Soviets out of the war. But Soviet premier Joseph Stalin had already made a commitment to the United States to enter the conflict. Thus the first atomic raid on Japan was scheduled for August 6.

On August 3, Truman left Potsdam and boarded the *Augusta*. While

The Decision to Drop the Bomb (inset: Fred Freed, producer). Courtesy of Films Incorporated

at sea, he met with the press, exclaiming, "Well, boys, I'm going to scoop you again. We're going to drop an atom bomb on Japan and we're going to end this war in less than ninety days."[6]

Atomic bombs were dropped on Hiroshima and Nagasaki on August 6 and 9 respectively, at the cost of nearly 150,000 Japanese lives. The war lasted less than thirty days after the bombing. Japan, despite violent reprisals by some military fanatics, finally surrendered.

In the United States, antiemperor feelings ran high. Many members of the Congress referred to Hirohito as a war criminal, while others favored measures ranging from execution to hanging him by his toes.[7] But the majority of our leaders favored the Japanese keeping the emperor in power. The reaction in America over the atomic explosions seemed to be overshadowed by the fact that the war had come to an end.

There has been much debate over the moral justification of dropping bombs of such force on live targets. President Truman repeatedly voiced his convictions. In a television interview with Edward R. Murrow on 2 February 1958, Murrow asked the president if he had any regrets about his decision. Replied Truman: "not the slightest in the world. None of us want war and all of us are against war, but when you have the weapon that will win the war you'd be foolish if you didn't use it."[8] A year later, on 28 April 1959, at Columbia University, Truman stated, "it was the same as getting a bigger gun than the other fellow had to win the war. That's what it was used for, nothing else but an artillery weapon."[9]

Research by Giovanitti and Freed suggests that not only Truman but men such as Secretary of War Henry L. Stimson, Dr. J. Robert Oppenheimer, James F. Byrnes, and General Groves were also instrumental in the decision to drop the bomb. Truman was merely one lever in the vast governmental machinery that, when pushed, started the mechanism. According to Freed, however, Truman eventually made the ultimate decision, even though he did not know about the bomb until he became president.

Freed spent many hours interviewing members of the congressional committees and military men in order to obtain answers to specific questions. Concise editing enabled Chet Huntley, the narrator, to obtain direct answers to his questions. The editing process for *Decision* is perhaps best explained by David Yellin in his book: *Special: Fred Freed and the Television Documentary*. Yellin says, "Freed will rarely shoot less than 50,000 feet of film. The usual one-hour documentary requires about 2,000 feet of film for the show. In a heavy interview show such as *The Decision to Drop the Bomb* he can go as high as a 50–1 ratio or 100,000 feet of film."[10] Because the documentary *Decision* was a ninety-minute program, Freed spent nine months in production. His editing was more effective because he had ample footage, enabling him to be more selective.

Freed's questions all seem to have a designated purpose. It is interesting to consider how he was able to approach the interviewees twenty years after the bombings. At first, he read all the books, documents, and newspaper stories he could about the subject. Then he began to consult with experts about his documentary. He spoke with them at great length before attempting to shoot a foot of film. He first discovered what they knew; information that was not available in texts or the public record. Eventually he reached the film interview. But only after being satisfied that the subject matter had been thoroughly explored did the cameras begin recording.

Of the several emotional responses elicited from the film, one of the most memorable was unrehearsed. Freed asked Dr. Oppenheimer to describe his feelings on seeing the first atomic explosion. The scientist replied: "We knew the world would not be the same. Few people laughed. Few people cried. Most people were silent. I remembered the line from the Hindu scripture the *Bhagavad Gita*: Vishnu is trying to persuade the prince that he should do his duty, and to impress him, takes on his multi-armed form and says 'Now I am become death, destroyer of worlds.'"[11] At the exact moment Oppenheimer quoted Vishnu, the camera zoomed in for a close-up and a tear came to Oppenheimer's eye.

With every interview, Freed knew exactly the role each man would play in the documentary. To insure accuracy, he permitted the interviewees to use notes. General Groves, who headed the Manhattan Project, which built the atomic bomb, was an informational witness. Some questions to Groves were stated as follows: "Look, General, what we're after is everything you know about this particular point. What were you thinking when you made decisions about which Japanese cities would be targets?"[12] After each question the general was given time to think and sort out his answer. Then, and only then, did Freed permit the cameras to roll.

Most documentaries offer some dramatization of subject matter while conveying intended messages. One of the film's most powerful moments occurs when the camera pans over the ruins of Hiroshima—there is complete silence. Only the sound of wind was added to create an impression of desolation and loneliness.[13] In the distance the figure of a forlorn person on a bicycle, barely visible, is seen moving from the right to the left of the screen in the panoramic view of the ruins. A symbol of solitude is created.

Freed's imagery has a definite purpose. In the first part of the film, there were several aerial shots of bombed Japanese cities, signifying widespread devastation. Almost simultaneously, aerial photography of the United States Pentagon appears. The scenes suggest the power structure of the Allies and their growing strength. It also poses a question—why use the bomb on a near-defeated nation? Other vivid scenes of imagery were those of the Imperial Palace. During the film (stock footage), the narrator emphasizes the dichotomy between Japanese political and military leaders. Whenever there were shots of bombed Japanese cities, films of B-29s dropping their loads, or passages implying danger to Japan, Freed would cut to scenes of the Imperial Palace. Sound effects of chirping birds create a peaceful impression. No one person was ever seen in these pictures, giving viewers the impression that while leaders were quarreling behind the tranquil setting of palace walls, their nation was crumbling. Prior to witnessing the final destruction of Hiroshima and Nagasaki, phrases are extracted from Secretary Stimson's diary of 1946: "The face of war is the face of death. . . . War in this century has grown more barbarous, especially now with the release of atomic energy. . . . We must never have another war; there is no other choice."

For years critics have asked, "Did the United States have an alternative for using the bomb?" In his book, Freed says that our armed forces conducted fire raids from the air and developed blockades to induce starvation as possible alternatives. Freed leaves the question open for debate. Near the film's conclusion he subtly suggests the atomic bomb was not "necessary" to win the war. This point of view is presented pictorially by concentrating his imagery on the ruins of Japan's cities that were destroyed by conventional weapons.

It is to Freed's credit, however, that most possible alternatives leading to the final decision are presented. His factual background material is exceedingly well documented.

He asks, for example, whether the dropping of the bomb was purely a political decision. Initially, it was a military operation, but Freed supports the thesis that politics played a significant role in the final decision. He constantly mentions the bomb was kept secret from our Allies. The possibility of wartime alliances breaking up and an arms race occurring are examined. The fear of the Soviet Union led Freed to surmise that the dropping of the bombs was a deliberate demonstration of power to be witnessed by the Allies, especially the Russians.

Although not mentioned in the documentary, the decision to "use" the bomb in some way was imminent from the moment Roosevelt ordered its construction. Once two billion dollars had been appropriated, one could assume the end product would be used in some way. Most of the debate in the documentary focused on whether the bomb should have been used on live Japanese targets, but the use was never in doubt. It appears those who strongly supported the decision did so because they could see no alternative to using the weapon—we were at war.

Producing a documentary on the decision to employ atomic bombs and attempting to maintain objectivity is a difficult task. Peter Watkins, the director-producer of *The War Game* believes objectivity in a film about atomic warfare is unrealistic.[14] His documentary on nuclear war was subjective; thus, primarily in Great Britain, he received severe criticism for presenting only his views. He was accused of being too harshly realistic and for propagandizing in favor of nuclear disarmament. Watkins's purpose was to offer his film from a subjective viewpoint, and this he did. Fred Freed, however, honestly endeavored to achieve objectivity; the events of 1945 as they actually happened. Freed claims documentary films should function as a social lie detector, and one cannot produce a good documentary on a false premise.[15] His *Decision to Drop the Bomb* is successful in offering viewers a realistic and purposeful reminder that our civilization has the power to destroy itself.

One significant question raised in his documentary was, should one man or any select group of men have the power to make a decision of such importance? The conclusion is left to the viewer. But Freed also revealed how each man working with the project experienced the pain of science, human frustration, and limited foresight. It was apparent most men were frightened of using the bomb. Their anguish over the consequences of not using the bomb was also shown. Constant references to a possible American invasion of Japan, perhaps similar to D day, one million American casualties, Japan's steadfast refusal to surrender, and a two-billion-dollar appropriation were factors that each scientist was forced to consider. Freed suggests that those men making the decision were peaceful, dedicated men, similar to ourselves. Possessing human strengths and weaknesses, they were caught up in a world of transition. A world war had to be ended. The nation was clamoring for peace. New world powers were emerging.

The Decision to Drop the Bomb neither condemns nor pardons the men, it merely reflects the facts, as seen by producer Fred Freed, as they were. The documentary has significance not only to those who lived through the decisions of 1944–45 but to today's generation as well. Young Americans have little conception of four years of world war. Freed offers them and others documented segments of events in history that altered the course of our lives.

15

DAVID G. YELLIN

Countdown to Zero

In a special interview for this text, Professor David Yellin discusses the making of *Countdown to Zero* with the late award-winning documentary film producer, Fred Freed.

DAVID G. YELLIN: We agreed when we were working on the text, *Special: Fred Freed and the Television Documentary*, that *Countdown to Zero* was not one of your better documentaries. We also thought that although the program was disappointing, it was important to your development as a documentary film maker. You learned something about journalism, history, world politics, network politics, nuclear power, and your own prejudices. Actually this documentary, perhaps because it failed, is a good one to probe. A postmortem. To ascertain if television documentarians, like ordinary mortals, learn from their mistakes.

FRED FREED: I certainly learned from *Countdown*. But after reviewing this show as you and I have, David, *Countdown* wasn't as bad as I originally thought. It just wasn't as good as I hoped it would be.

YELLIN: Then what we're going to attempt here, Fred, is to find out why it wasn't what you hoped it would be. Let's start at the beginning. Why did you choose to produce this show in 1966?

FREED: At that time, there was much talk about the proliferation of nuclear weapons. Five nations (United States, Russia, England, France, China) had the bomb. The big question was how many more would join this atomic club? Twenty? Forty? It seemed a logical *White Paper* show for us to develop. I had done the one on Hiroshima, *The Decision to Drop the Bomb*, a year before (5 January 1965). Immediately afterward I produced a three-and-a-half-hour foreign policy show (*United States Foreign Policy*, 7 September 1965). Basically, our foreign policy since Hiroshima had been built around our nuclear position. Also, my book with associate producer and director, Len Giovannitti (*The Decision to Drop the Bomb: A Political History*), had just been published. So it seemed important to me to update the nuclear story. There was so much dialogue about Israel and India making their own atomic weapons—some believed Israel already had them. If Israel had atomic weapons, then the Arabs would want to have them. And the only place they could get them would be the Soviet Union.

YELLIN: If India joined the nuclear club, it was thought Pakistan would too, by either building its own bomb or obtaining nuclear weapons from China. The question of Japan, Australia, and Indonesia, all of which *could* build the bomb, was then given consideration.

FREED: That was the conventional wisdom.

YELLIN: The conventional wisdom was that if Israel or India received nuclear weapons, then other countries—which could conceivably build them—would?

FREED: Correct. In 1966, it was obvious that almost anybody could make a bomb. As Ralph Lapp, an American physicist, said on *Countdown*, "the bomb is very easy to make, very inexpensive." He noted that a bomb, equal to the one dropped on Hiroshima, could be made for only a million dollars. Lapp has continued his campaign since appearing on our program. He's even suggesting the Mafia may make bombs. I think in the mid-sixties people didn't understand, including ourselves when we were doing the show, that in a nuclear age it would be better not to be burdened with nuclear weapons nor to be burdened with a giant military establishment. There are other, better ways of spending money. Germany and Japan, both of which don't have large armed forces, have become great economic powers in the world; and economic power is what matters. The Saudi Arabians are not noted for their armed forces, but they are going to have a powerful world voice because they have oil.

YELLIN: But in September of 1965, when you started working on *Countdown*, you had a different view of the meaning of nuclear proliferation on the world scene. Chet Huntley said in his opening narration, as he stood looking out of a window with a view of the New York skyline: "In the next hour we are going to talk about what no one wants to talk about; to think about the unthinkable."

FREED: Yes. We were thinking about the possibilities of nuclear confrontation and what might happen if ten or twenty nations had atomic power. This could create a situation in which, as Chet said, "It [New York City] and all the other cities of the United States could be totally wiped out twenty-two minutes from the pushing of a button on the other side of the world." But that is tabloid thinking about the unthinkable. *Countdown* didn't have the journalistic or scholarly qualities of *The Decision to Drop the Bomb*. It never went behind the headlines. That's one major fault of the show. We didn't start out to do it that way, but we did it that way. That's why it was one of the most unsatisfactory documentaries I ever produced.

YELLIN: But you had everything going for you, that is, everything you had on your other more successful shows. You had six months to prepare, it was your first program in color, and you had sufficient funds. You went some $30,000 over your then sufficiently generous $120,000 budget. You had expert advisors in international politics, including eight NBC foreign correspondents, and you had access to nuclear experts such as Herman Kahn, director of the Hudson Institute, Ralph Lapp, General Gallois, the French nuclear theoretician, and many other world scholars, diplomats, political leaders, and disarmament proponents. What went wrong?

FREED: A failure of reporting. We didn't investigate with any depth. The real feeling of those countries without the bomb wasn't carefully analyzed as to whether they were actually going to build it. We overemphasized the idea of German militarism, accepting the idea that Germans were militarists because they had always been. We didn't understand that Germans of the next generation were more interested in survival and prosperity. We simply accepted the conventional wisdom. Then we looked at India and said, "You know India's going to make the bomb because they're afraid Pakistan might get one from China." We failed to observe that India and Pakistan were so economically weak they couldn't afford the bomb, nor did they really want it. I think, looking back on it, it was simply a failure of reporting.

YELLIN: Could you have explained every country's problems to an American television audience? Would you have been more objective if you had, as you did in *Decision*, ninety minutes of air time?

FREED: No.

YELLIN: Then you had too much to report?

FREED: I don't know. I do know *Countdown* should have been better produced.

YELLIN: Perhaps you shouldn't have done it. It was too complicated.

FREED: We should have. And we could have. The fault was that I felt so strongly this was going to happen, this threat of spreading nuclear weapons, that we might all be destroyed. We had to do something about it quickly and I didn't stop to question whether my own assumptions—no matter how logical they appeared to be—were true.

YELLIN: What you're owning up to, Fred, is your own bias, your own predetermined conclusions got you into a difficult situation.

FREED: That's right. This is why I am against advocacy journalism. I was deeply involved. I had lived, in a sense, with the bomb since my first *White Paper: Khrushchev and Berlin* (26 December 1961), followed by *The Missile Crisis* (9 February 1964) and, of course, *Decision* and *Foreign Policy*. So, when I approached *Countdown*, I was an advocate. I had seen nuclear politics in action and truly felt there would be a proliferation of nuclear weapons. And I believed that proliferation had to be stopped. If one television program could help, and if my program could strike a nerve somewhere, it was important to do it. And so I did it as an advocate and not as a journalist.

YELLIN: Your objection to advocacy journalism seems to be that it is limiting. Does it stop you from going beyond your own point of view? Is it especially limiting when the conventional wisdom confirms your own point of view?

FREED: Yes. I always get the feeling I'm asking the right questions not only when I question other people's assumptions but also—and even more so—when I begin to question my own assumptions. With *Countdown* I did not question my own assumptions. If I had, perhaps it would have been better television. But our responsibility in doing this documentary—in every documentary we produce—is to try and find out how things really are, as opposed to how people think they are. Our purpose is simply to inform as well and as thoroughly as we can. And we failed with *Countdown*.

YELLIN: I think in this case you're being too critical of yourself.

FREED: Self-flagellation is absolutely necessary. I think too often documentary producers on network television begin thinking that the truth of the world is in their hands. And that's not true. I believe you should suffer for your errors. My failure is not that I was unable to discover the right answers, the failure came in not having pursued it through questioning the conventional wisdom.

YELLIN: The irony here is that most reviewers praised the program. In New York, Harriet Van Horne said it was "cool, calm and terrifying

. . . deserves to be repeated not once but many times this year." Percy Shain, the Boston reviewer, called it "an important and studious contribution to what should be a prime concern of mankind." Philadelphia critic Harry Harris said you wrote "a chilling report."

FREED: Yes, I still have those reviews.

YELLIN: Jack Gould (*New York Times*) called it "agonizingly familiar" and "useful but dated." He was the only one who didn't like it. But most critics gave you good-to-rave reviews.

FREED: Those reviewers liked it because what we said sustained the conventional wisdom of the time. And Gould didn't accept it because he thought it too obvious and trite.

YELLIN: What about your relations on *Countdown* with the executives at NBC? At the time you began *Countdown*, Julian Goodman was second in command at NBC News. It's interesting to note, though it doesn't have any direct bearing on our discussion, that in April of 1966, Julian Goodman had already surpassed several executives to replace Robert E. Kintner as president of the company.

FREED: On *Countdown*, I worked from the beginning with Julian. He was the only one who saw it before it was aired. Julian didn't like the idea of *Countdown* from the very beginning; he thought that I could not tell that story, that it was too dull, abstract, a secret story in a sense—the people who knew the secret wouldn't, couldn't, talk about it. He felt there was no way of knowing whether Israel was going to build the bomb. There was no way of getting behind the scenes and talking to people who knew the truth. Or, if you did locate them, they wouldn't tell you. It wasn't like *Decision*, when we spoke with many of the principals twenty years after the fact; they were anxious to get their versions on record. Julian didn't think the same drama could emerge by probing Israel about whether they should build the bomb.

YELLIN: Yet he allowed you to go ahead with the film? Why?

FREED: I'm not sure. Probably because I convinced him the program was important.

YELLIN: Well, you not only went over the budget some 25 percent, but—and I guess we can say this now—you had a ball doing this show.

FREED: That's true. I traveled to Paris, Geneva, London, and all over the United States. Bob Garland, the associate producer, went to India, Israel, Egypt, and Pakistan. We were in constant touch with each other. Occasionally, it was similar to cloak-and-dagger episodes. Especially in Israel—we secretly got the first pictures of their nuclear reactor at

Dimona. One of our cameramen sneaked into the area and with a long-range lens photographed it.

YELLIN: Were you able to convince Nasser of the United Arab Republic to be on the program?

FREED: When we first approached Nasser, he said absolutely no. That is, his aides said, "If you have any Israelis on it, the President won't do it." We went back and forth for some time; finally, we said, "The Israelis are saying this and that, and we're going to say, on the air, that Egypt said, 'We have no answer.'" This technique usually doesn't work, but in this case, it did and Nasser was interviewed. But the show still didn't work.

YELLIN: You've said it wasn't successful for several reasons. You didn't do a good job of reporting. You accepted without question the conventional wisdom, and you were too much the advocate. But, let's see if there are other reasons. For instance, it might have been because of the subject matter. After all, it was a broad subject. You were investigating a topic that could affect our civilization.

FREED: We talked about the same thing in *Decision*, and it worked.

YELLIN: Exactly. Why? Why *Decision* and not *Countdown*?

FREED: In *Decision*, we did something original. We went to the sources and described, for the first time on television, how the decision-making process of the American government functioned. We showed that in government, once a decision is made to move in any direction, there is an inevitability about it, an inability to stop it once it begins moving, an inability to analyze it dispassionately once all the various factions start acting. It's like a snowball rolling down a hill. That's why I think *Decision* was so valuable. I showed that it wasn't a deliberate wickedness that authorized the bomb to drop on Hiroshima. I'm not sure whether it was the right or wrong decision, but it was not made by men who rationally examined the whole picture. The decision was made by various groups who had different reasons at different times. It was made by some who said, "We spent two billion dollars on it, we can't stop," or "If we don't use it, and we invade Japan and millions of our boys are killed, we'll be blamed," or "We've got to show the Russians." Probably the best explanation came from Dr. Robert Oppenheimer, who said: "The decision was implicit in the project. I don't know whether it could have been stopped."

YELLIN: In *Countdown*, you weren't able to create that same thoroughness, the inevitability in the decisions of various nonnuclear club countries as to whether they were going to build the bomb.

FREED: Mostly because it wasn't there. We thought it was, but we were wrong. In 1966, nuclear war was unthinkable. The great powers, especially the United States and Russia, were not prepared to risk total destruction for any cause. But the conventional wisdom in 1966 said smaller nations would argue, "You are our ally, and we're going to use it against anybody who threatens us, and what are you going to do?" Or they would offer rationalizations similar to France when they joined the atomic club, saying, "This is a deterrent." But it wasn't a deterrent. Nine bombs could destroy France, and Russia could unleash nine hundred on France before the United States could do anything about it. In *Decision*, we told people something they didn't know about history. In *Countdown*, we were dealing with the future, and we tended to mislead people into believing something was going to happen, which didn't.

YELLIN: I agree, Fred. In *Countdown*, you started out with Chet Huntley saying (voice over) against shots of Hiroshima bomb, Minuteman missile in silo, missile fires, New York building dusk, New York skyline: "Twenty-seven hundred United States missiles and bombs are ready to fire every hour, day and night. Almost as many are pointed at United States citizens." And the documentary concluded with Chet Huntley intoning: "There are, in the arsenals of the nuclear powers, warheads with the equivalent of ten tons of TNT for every man, woman and child on earth. . . . It would take about twenty minutes, by the clock, for a missile launched from the farthest point across the world to reach any American city." The last shot we see is the New York skyline at night, and, as you super the credits, we hear: *Clock ticking.* Obviously a scare tactic. What else might you have done? You honestly were afraid of the world's future because of what you thought you knew.

FREED: I was wrong. And it's my responsibility not to be wrong. I don't think we needed to scare anybody. We needed to go beyond that kind of obviousness and present the facts. There is a positive side of *Countdown*. I've learned from my mistakes. In making the first of two defense programs in early 1973 ("NBC Reports": *And When the War Is Over—The American Military in the 70's*), we were better. In *War Is Over* all of those nuclear weapons are there, with the same potential of total destruction. This time, we showed that villains are neither nuclear weapons nor officers manning them but rather society, which is unable to say "Stop." In *War Is Over*, we made the officers human beings. We showed they are just sons, brothers, friends, neighbors, people like us. And they're responsible for these terrible weapons—reading books, thinking, and half going out of their minds just sitting there with nuclear power. These men, and men like them, have been doing this for almost thirty years now—Americans, who are saying, "If you want us to stand down, tell us." But no one tells them. Both sides are locked in this insane death dance. This point was necessary to make, it had some validity, and it went beyond the conventional wisdom. Journalistically we asked the right questions and we informed people in an honest, useful manner. Throughout this I kept remembering *Countdown*.

YELLIN: Your producing *War Is Over* was similar of *Countdown*, a retribution? But this time, unlike in *Countdown to Zero*, you were in control of your material and not vice versa.

FREED: I think in any television documentary, you face the same decision-making problems as government officials. But it's the initial decision that sets the inertia on its way. We know, David, the critical decision comes when you determine the point of view you're going to take. That is the single most important decision a documentary film producer must decide. It's not the point of view in terms of the political, but the angle of vision you are observing. You must always know your story line and how you're going to reveal it. That's the one decision from which you can never recover if you make the wrong one.

16 JACK G. SHAHEEN

The War Game

The War Game, a forty-seven-minute television documentary concerned with a hypothetical nuclear attack on Great Britain, was made available for theatrical distribution in 1966 and was awarded an Oscar as Best Feature Documentary for that year. Following the initial screening of The War Game, Kenneth Tynan wrote, in the National Observer, "The War Game may be the most important film ever made. We are always being told that a work of art cannot change the course of history; I think this one might. It should be screened everywhere on earth."[1] Yet, as of this writing, The War Game produced for the British Broadcasting Corporation has not appeared on any television screen in Britain, the United States, or anywhere else in the world. Nor is it likely to.

Although the documentary is one of the most impassioned outcries against nuclear warfare yet to be conveyed on film, it will probably continue to receive only limited exposure. Unlike previous attempts to portray atomic war, such as Fail Safe, On the Beach, Dr. Strangelove, and The Bedford Incident, The War Game illustrates what happens to the population immediately after the bomb explodes. With most films, the final reel stops when the blue flash ignites.

Interestingly, the documented newsreels of Hiroshima and Nagasaki, excerpts of films taken by Japanese photographers showing the effects of nuclear war on Japan, have been shown on television. These newsreels, however, were classified by the United States military authorities and banned from all public viewing until 1968. The significance of Peter Watkins's The War Game and why it remains banned from television screens in this nuclear age merit analysis. The purpose of this analysis is twofold: to explicate the film and to discuss why it has not been aired.

The hypothetical situation posed in *The War Game* has the United States threatening to use atomic weapons against Chinese troops that have entered South Vietnam. Russia then announces that unless the weapons are withdrawn, it will take over West Berlin. Riots erupt at Checkpoint Charlie. When NATO divisions moving across East Germany meet superior Russian forces, the West counters with tactical nuclear weapons. Russia responds by attacking Western Europe with atomic missiles. But the thermonuclear missiles aimed at military installations in Britain fall short of their mark and descend on the civilian population of the County of Kent.

In simulated cinéma vérité, *The War Game* reveals a world of unrelieved horror. The imminence of nuclear warfare comes first in the frantic evacuation plans to rush children, pregnant women, and the sick to places of safety—there are not enough shelters. Firestorms, similar to those that occurred in World War II over Dresden, Hamburg, and Darmstadt, suck up the oxygen on earth and leave firemen and civilian defense workers breathing only carbon gases. Police aid physicians by putting the hopelessly wounded out of their misery with shotguns. Transportation facilities are not adequate to remove the corpses.[2]

There are excellent visual aspects of this film. A particularly impressive yet realistic instance of personal tragedy comes near the film's conclusion when Watkins pans his camera in close-up along the endless rows of blackened corpses and then pulls the camera up and back to reveal a family group, also black and motionless, sitting on a curb at the end of a row of bodies. For approximately fifteen seconds, the father, mother, son, and daughter are a tableau of death—the daughter then makes a small flicker of movement, and she pulls on her mother's sleeve for comfort. The mother does not respond; the rejected child ceases her feeble action to rejoin her wax-figure family.[3] This scene brings to mind a particularly ominous device that Watkins uses to end certain scenes in the film. Instead of the expected dissolve or fade out, selected frames are frozen in a photograph, giving a memorial tone to the victims. The detailed realism, the information the narrator endlessly supplies, the wax-figure family and the freeze-frame technique somehow suggest that what the viewer sees may have happened.

Watkins does not use professional actors; a cross-section of the residents of Kent was engaged for purposes of achieving realism. Although

The War Game. Courtesy of Contemporary Films/McGraw-Hill

he spent two years reading hundreds of books on the subject of nuclear war and had lengthy discussions with people who thought the bomb should be employed if necessary (men in the church, civil defense experts, biophysicists, painters, writers, men in communication, and men of letters), he appears to be strongly influenced by John Hershey's book *Hiroshima*—for example, this excerpt of *Hiroshima*—

> As Mrs. Nakamura stood watching her neighbor, everything flashed whiter than any white she had ever seen. . . . She had taken a single step. . . . when something picked her up and she seemed to fly into the next room over the raised sleeping platform, pursued by parts of her house.
>
> Timbers fell around her as she landed. . . . The debris did not cover her deeply. . . . She heard a child cry, "Mother, help me!" and saw her youngest, the five year old, buried up to his breast and unable to move. As Mrs. Nakamura started frantically to claw her way toward the baby, she could see or hear nothing of her other children.[4]

Then this sequence from *The War Game*: "I saw a mother and child come down the street—and there was a terrific gust of wind, and the child was sucked out of his mother's grasp and into the flames."[5]

To enhance his vision of reality, Watkins constantly focuses the camera on the faces of Kent's citizens. Shades of gray prevail in this black and white film; all facial expressions seem predestined to eventually blur out; subtle refracted light tones tend only to mar blackened, pained physiognomies of the victims.

Watkins asks whether the survivors will envy the dead—will those citizens of Kent and their children who escaped death ever be the same? Today, the survivors of Hiroshima and Nagasaki face a variety of medical problems (stomach cancer, burns, loss of hair, glaucoma, and the decrease of the white corpuscles), not to mention the psychological problems. The victims' children experience medical abnormalities and suffer anxieties about marriage and employment.[6]

Dr. Robert Jay Lifton of Yale University in his text *Death in Life: Survivors of Hiroshima*, writes, "Being exposed to the atomic bomb just for an instant in time led to a lifelong encounter with death."[7] The experience, notes Dr. Lifton, stayed with the survivors throughout their lives and remains with them even now. He cites four basic stages: 1) the exposure to the bomb and the sea of death in which they found themselves at that time; 2) the acute radiation symptoms that occur days and weeks after the bomb; 3) years later, the increased incidents of some forms of leukemia and cancer, which reactivated vivid images of death; 4) finally, a lifelong identity with the dead.

The Japanese survivors carry with them, adds Lifton, a continuing imagery of death that can never be eradicated.[8] This same imagery is apparent when viewing Watkins's survivors of the Kent explosions. A bronze statue of a teacher protecting his students was recently unveiled in Hiroshima. The statue is a memorial to more than two thousand unidentified pupils and teachers who died in the atomic holocaust. The very essence of Dr. Lifton's text is poignant: nuclear war is not any war, it is a special hell. Peter Watkins produced *The War Game* because of "the possibility of nuclear war. There is no happy ending. I made it because I believe there is a silence on why we possess nuclear weapons. It is not a ban-the-bomb film. We don't *ask* anymore, we don't criticize. We accept. I wanted to make the man in the street stop to think about himself and the future." [9]

It is somewhat of a paradox that the BBC, noted for its freedom and liberal thought, would finance the film, then refuse to release it because it was "too horrifying." As Bertrand Russell notes, "Those who try to make you uneasy by talk about atom bombs are regarded as trouble-makers, . . . as people who spoil the pleasure of a fine day by foolish prospects of an improbable rain." The BBC was critical, saying the document was a fatalistic, bitter, hopeless, and cruel film, lacking any compassion and unsuitable for family viewing.

In a personal interview with Mrs. Winifred Crum Ewing, producer of documentaries for the BBC, the author asked Mrs. Ewing if she agreed with the BBC decision. She replied:

> Well, I have great sympathy with the BBC, having commissioned *The War Game* and then refusing to show it. There's no difficulty in seeing *The War Game* if you want to see it. . . . But, having lived in the Southeast of England throughout the war, having seen how people behave in circumstances of war and bombing, it was an absolute slander on humanity. His observations were profoundly wrong. . . . this is not the way people behave toward each other in times of stress. . . . I think it was a *stinking* film. We don't need these emotional, left-wing intellectuals to tell us that we can destroy the world.
>
> When I see a film like *The War Game*, I am ashamed of it, and I think the BBC was quite right to ban it. And I hope, shown in a country like this where you have not got the personal experience of seeing how ordinary people react to an extraordinary situation, that you will not believe that this is true. I'm not a left-wing intellectual, am I?[10]

Watkins disagrees: "If I had made a film about nuclear war and people either laughed at it or had I made Britain's recovery from that war quite firm and the Union Jack fluttered on the non-radioactive breeze, I have no doubt the film would have been shown. I must emphasize that it was because there is a feeling of hopelessness at the end that the film was banned." [11]

When the BBC initially announced that *The War Game* would not be on television (the first film ever banned by the corporation), it quickly added there had been no outside influence. A labor minister of Parliament, however, hinted to the press that pressure was a deciding factor. Watkins immediately resigned from the corporation. He contacted political leaders and liberal columnists in what he describes as his own "controlled battle." Finally, the BBC made the film available for release—to the cinema. [12]

In 1966, the BBC's annual report stated that the corporation should not "confine itself to seeking the comfortable solution to safe programs that avoid saying anything provocative by virtually saying nothing new." [13] British irony was not intended. The BBC did produce the documentary. A bright young director employed by most television companies would never have bothered to propose such a project, and if he had, it probably would have been refused.

People know very little about the sophistication of weapon systems or the cobalt and neutron bombs. Yet if one asks any group of people if they believe there will be a thermonuclear war in their lifetime or in the lifetime of their children, they will probably reply, "Yes, there's a chance." [14]

Mr. John E. Davis, the U.S. director of National Civil Defense, was asked by National Public Radio reporter, Jim Russell, if the American people consider the possibility of a Hiroshima on our soil; said Davis, "I think back in the conscience there's a knowledge that there's a possibility of it. On the other hand it's horrendous enough, the catastrophe is so bad that they don't want to think about it." [15] Davis added, "I think people generally realize the futility of the rise of nuclear weapons. On the other hand, we can't tell, at least history hasn't borne it out—that they wouldn't be used." [16]

Peter Watkins advocates a balanced discussion in all areas of public media, press, television, and radio about what the thermonuclear balance of terror is, what the bomb is, why we have it, and where the system is likely to go wrong. It may be possible at the end of such discussions that decisions on the viability of the bomb will be based on knowledge. The cause of our current situation, says Watkins, seems to be programmed ignorance, ignorance on what the bomb is, and ignorance as to why we have it.

Through knowledge man may have an opportunity to infiltrate those systems which perpetuate the employment of nuclear stockpiling. Hopefully, the charred, frightened faces of children in *The War Game*, which resemble authentic ikons of a Hiroshima to come, will serve as a reminder; everything that happens to Watkins's anonymous nonprofessional actors has happened to someone, somewhere in our time. The film is not science fiction.[17] Serious consideration might be given to Dwight MacDonald's suggestion: "Were I a Congressman, God forbid, I'd introduce a bill making it compulsory for all Senators and Representatives plus all administration officials whose offices are carpeted to attend a special screening of *The War Game*. Absence would be punishable by one year in jail or $1,000 fine or both. . . . the Supreme Court would have to throw out my bill on constitutional grounds: cruel and unusual punishment."[18]

Watkins's documentary is extremely significant. Live interviews mixed with carefully staged vignettes; quotes from military, scientific, and religious authorities; and the grainy newsreel quality of the cinematography create an almost-authentic vision of nuclear catastrophe. Although Watkins was criticized for failing to depict the resilience of the human spirit, his documentary has a cumulative emotional and educational effect. It reveals the threat of an atomic holocaust is always with us.[19]

The year following the bombings of Hiroshima and Nagasaki, and twenty years before *The War Game* was produced, Stephen Vincent Benét wrote,

> Oh, where are you coming from, soldier, gaunt soldier,
> With weapons beyond any reach of my mind,
> With weapons so deadly the world must grow older
> And die in its tracks, if it does not turn kind?[20]

Benét's effective commentary enhances the importance of *The War Game*; we are reminded of what the consequences of an atomic game could be.

17

**JACK G. SHAHEEN
AND EUGENE M. URAM**

Footnotes on the
Atomic Age

Footnotes on the Atomic Age, a documentary featured on
NBC's "First Tuesday" series, is journalistic overkill. The choice of
music, stock footage, and editing style create inappropriate witticisms
instead of newsworthy information. The program opens with an attempt
at sarcasm—the *Dr. Strangelove* song, Vera Lynn's "Someday We'll
Meet Again," is visually accompanied by a black and white montage
of exploding A-bombs. There are soft dissolves of mushroom clouds
billowing in the desert air, as subtitles appear, giving the date and
names of atomic test explosions from 1946 to 1952 (Test Able, Test
Baker, and Operation Ivy). The documentary concludes with a colorful
atomic explosion, while Peggy Lee sings, "Is That All There Is?"

The musical selections which appear at the beginning and end provide a slanted perspective concerning the possible peaceful uses of the
atom. Totally lacking in continuity, *Footnotes* is mainly comprised of
editorial ramblings by reporter Tom Pettit. Pettit fails to document the
complex issues from a balanced perspective. He offers instead a superficial overview of numerous topics; the danger of atomic fallout, the
effects of atomic testing in Alaska, Colorado, New Mexico, and Nevada, the ineptness of the private business sector and the potential threat
of nuclear reactors in foreign nations. Also, stock footage is used to
depict the Atomic Energy Commission as an insensitive and inefficient
organization.

The documentary first reveals the problems of fallout by focusing
on army veteran Patrick Stout. Pettit notes that on 9 September 1945,
Stout stood for twelve minutes at ground zero in Alamogordo, New
Mexico, the site of the first nuclear explosion of the same year. Stout,

a member of the United States Army's investigative unit, on seeing the blast wrote, "I shall never forget the sight . . . as long as I live." In the spring of 1967, Stout became very ill and was diagnosed as having leukemia. On 29 January 1969, after several appeals, he was granted disability compensation. A final appeal board conceded that "service connection" caused the leukemia; on 18 April 1969, he died.

The edited case history of Patrick Stout is a touching prelude. Stout, notes Pettit, is only one example of what might have happened to reporters and soldiers who visited ground zero only two months following the initial explosions. Literally thousands of armed forces personnel were transported to Nevada in 1951 and 1952. Stock footage shows that approximately five thousand servicemen, marines, and airborne troops, were engaged in "close-in operations" following the detonation of the Nevada bombs.

The footage suggests the men were in danger of being too close to the explosions, emphasizing the threat of radiation disease. Narrator Pettit says there has not been a follow-up study of these men, but he does not provide insight as to why no postanalysis was performed. Viewers are left with doubts as to whether the servicemen were affected.

Footnotes' peacetime explosive theme is taken from two Atomic Energy Commission (AEC) films, *Project Plowshare* and *Amchitka Revisited*. The films offer a positive view of nuclear bombs at work; with *Plowshare* graphics are used, suggesting the need for a new and wider Panama Canal. The action then shifts to a leading critic of the AEC emphatically stating, "That's foolish." Reporter Pettit imposes his comments over *Plowshare*'s narrator, contending the fate of tens of thousands of Panamanian Indians are at stake, and in Panama, the evidence is against a nuclear canal. During Pettit's comments, there are visuals of the Indians carrying a coffin.

Amchitka Revisited shows groups of children at play and paying tribute to the American flag. Their actions are accompanied by "America, the Beautiful." During these scenes the film's narrator states nuclear testing "must be a major priority." His comments are inappropriate and appear to be taken out of context.

By means of structural editorializing, *Footnotes* overdramatizes facts which, if left alone, would suffice to communicate intended meanings. By tampering with the AEC films, the documentary lessens its credibility.

Footnotes also relates an incident at Rocky Flats, Colorado, where a fire in a Dow plant caused the contamination of an entire plutonium operation. It is the most serious accident in the history of America's nuclear weapons program. Even the water used to fight the fire had to be decontaminated. There are excellent visuals of the fire cleanup operation which show decontamination crews in protective white garments checking personnel with geiger counters. Extreme care was taken as more than one-third of a million cubic feet of waste was moved to an undisclosed underground burial spot.

During the decontamination process, a plant fireman accidentally inhaled plutonium oxide. A reporter from an NBC affiliated station in Colorado interviewed the worker. He was virtually unconcerned about radiation illness mainly because of assurances given him by doctors. Yet the attending doctor, when repeatedly questioned by the reporter, somewhat reluctantly admitted the possibility of a cancerous tumor from the inhalation.

The film proceeds to mention that such tests continue to be carried out, under the protest of local citizens, at Amchitka; that Project Schooner (a nuclear hole-digging experiment) has, on two occasions, sent radioactive dust into the air, once as far away as Canada; that Project Plowshare is seriously considering the utilization of nuclear explosives to dig a new Panama Canal; and that Project Rulison (an unsuccessful attempt to mine natural gas by means of nuclear warheads) was carried out by a private firm despite protests of the inhabitants of nearby Aspen, Colorado.

The film draws the conclusion that peacetime experiments with the bomb for nonmilitary purposes are not only dangerous but nonproductive. Commenting on an atomic underground test blast that created a huge cavern, Pettit says: "That's all well and good, but what do you do with a big cavern?" In another scene where natural gas is squeezed out from an underground cavern it is discovered the gas is so radioactive it cannot be activated. Notes Pettit, "If you build a bomb according to fact, it will go off." The legacy of peacetime testing, suggests Pettit, is rubble.

Project Schooner hoped to prove that atomic bombs could dig deep trenches. It was discovered, however, that nuclear hole-digging emits radioactive dust into the air. *Footnotes* refers to one specific test on 8 December 1968, which sent radioactive particles into Utah, Montana, and Canada. The Canadian incident, says Pettit, was a clear-cut violation of the Nuclear Test Ban Treaty, a violation that has never been formally acknowledged by the United States. Thus, peacetime experiments have resulted in developing dormant radioactive caverns, caves, holes, and gas.

A third point made by *Footnotes* is the development of a seemingly laissez faire attitude about the bomb, exemplified by a business-as-usual stance of the AEC. Nuclear testing is described by the commission as a dynamic and viable industry that involves $225 million annually and employs four thousand people. The AEC stresses normal, routine testing of two nuclear warheads monthly and finds its operation to be "just like any business." At Rocky Flats, where $20 million of plutonium was destroyed and $45 million spent in decontamination, a government spokesman played down the possibility of further danger and compared the production of plutonium to automotive assemblage. And, at Project Rulison, a nuclear bomb was delivered by two unmarked trucks escorted by a sheriff's car to a private firm after having been transported over public highways. "It was as routine as a morning milk delivery," said Pettit. Displayed in public and for motion picture cameras were secret warheads that had previously been seen only by individuals with special security clearance. The bomb was described by a company spokesman as an effectual machine and hailed as a useful peacetime explosive.

Both the AEC and big business apparently view nuclear experimentation as a business—this is the fourth point made by *Footnotes*. AEC's Project Rulison, notes Pettit, is "another spectacular hole-digging exercise." In Colorado, Rulison was classified as a joint United States government-Austral Oil Company project. On 6 August 1969 (twenty-four years to the day after the Hiroshima bombing), the government gave the bomb to Austral Oil Company without charge and provided $500 million worth of liability insurance. Local citizens were unable to halt the experiment. They met with company representatives and objected strongly to paying for 10 percent of the experiment through tax money as well as paying for the gas if and when it was released. Representatives of Austral spoke glowingly of the peaceful use of wartime weapons; they also mentioned possible profits and risks.

Furthermore, the United States Joint Congressional Commission on Atomic Energy was seeking a new law that would permit the sale of atomic weapons commercially—provided there was government control and supervision. Interestingly, the United States government has been instrumental in providing nuclear reactors for various foreign governments. *Footnotes* shows footage of workers in India's plant, their reactor is used for peaceful applications. The reactors not only provide electricity but also ample amounts of plutonium that could produce between ten thousand and one hundred thousand nuclear weapons annually.

The final point made by the program is presented almost as an afterthought: Why is the government providing nuclear reactors to foreign agencies with personnel to operate them? If others can master the technology of the reactors, how long will it be before they learn to use plutonium and build their own bombs? These dangers are not thoroughly examined.

An initial study of the film indicates it yields much valuable information. But when examining *Footnotes* in relation to other documentaries, one discovers unwelcomed editorial inferences meriting analysis. A. William Bluem identifies and classifies television documentaries into distinct categories: the journalistic and the thematic. The journalistic documentary, Bluem says, is precise and impartial, and is not free to employ emotion-arousing devices. Conversely, the theme documentary is free to advance the subjective purpose of the poet and is idea dominated.[1]

Bluem also mentions the editorial documentary. Instead of having the film tell something, the editorial documentary is edited in such a manner to will something.[2] His discussion is revealing, especially regarding CBS's *Harvest of Shame* and NBC's *The Battle of Newburgh*. Of *Harvest of Shame*, Bluem said, "To be sure, there were interviews. . . . But these did not seek to balance . . . the presentation."[3] In *The Battle of Newburgh* an elder statesman of the city states "there are no simple answers to little problems." According to Bluem, those words brought *Newburgh* from editorializing and into the realm of impartial appraisal of great social needs.[4] The documentaries took a stand on controversial issues, recording on camera what had been observed.

Footnotes is an excellent example not only of editorial documentary but liberal meddling as well. Simple answers are offered to complex problems and there is little balanced editing of the interviews. Although vague points of view are established, the manner in which *Footnotes* is presented tends decidedly toward the emotional in lieu of the rational. It begins by focusing on former Secretary of Defense Robert McNamara; he warns about the dangers of nuclear testing. Edward Teller, one of the scientists who developed the hydrogen bomb, follows McNamara, and warns about the dangers of not testing. *Footnotes* then abruptly cuts from Teller's comments to footage taken from *Dr. Strangelove*; Vera Lynn sings "Someday We'll Meet Again" while bombs create collages of black and white clouds. (In Kubrick's film, it is the bespectacled, intellectual-looking President Mervin Muffley who is the voice of sanity, while the German-accented Dr. Strangelove delivers the voice of doom.)[5]

Footnotes uses this juxtaposition to editorialize. There appear to be physical comparisons between McNamara and Muffley, Teller and Strangelove. The arms race is vigorously supported by Teller (Dr. Strangelove) and countered by McNamara (President Muffley). Their opening statements may appear to be disconnected from the Vera Lynn song, but the editing is obviously intended to create similarities. This tone colors each developing scene. Thus the music editing at the film's beginning establishes an editorial bias. The camera cuts from Vera Lynn's singing to the accompaniment of exploding atomic bombs, to a cemetery where the family of Patrick Stout is seen visiting his grave-side. Has the fantasy become real? Through juxtaposition, the tone has been developed.

In *Footnotes*, Dr. Teller rarely appears trustworthy. He introduces the segment on the question of continuing nuclear experimentation—he speaks in favor of testing. His comments are immediately followed by statements from AEC spokesmen, asserting that nuclear experimentation is simply a business. McNamara follows, making a plea for a sane attitude toward nuclear stockpiling. Because of the editing structure, Teller's statements seem unreliable. Tom Pettit, for example, on introducing Teller, caustically describes the scientist as "the leading advocate of learning to love the bomb as a peaceful explosive." The editing creates two stereotyped groups—humanists and militarists. The humanists are McNamara, threatened citizens, infected workers, and Patrick Stout. The militarists are Teller, the Atomic Energy Commission, and big business—they are shown as having little concern for human life.

The AEC defends the peaceful use of plutonium abroad, but opposes the development of a technology that would employ plutonium as a destructive material. Successive film clips show Teller stating that it is fairly simple to make nuclear explosives, that such blasts could eventually create needed caverns, canals, and harbors. Narrator Pettit intones: "So far, at least, the nuclear bomb has no proven utility other than to explode." An AEC scientist then admits that in a year's time one nuclear reactor could produce enough potent plutonium to make up to one hundred thousand nuclear weapons. Suddenly, a bomb explodes to Peggy Lee's, "Is That All There Is?"

Footnotes is reminiscent of black comedy gone awry. Its complexity is difficult to analyze. Only a few segments contain evidence of no overt editorializing. The poignant investigation of the life and death of Patrick Stout personalizes the A-bomb experience. His struggle with leukemia is retold without being maudlin. Another example of factual reporting, unscarred by conscious editorializing, is the scene which details the plutonium fire at Rocky Flats. Here, the documentary is convincing, focusing on one of numerous problems facing those in the private sector who experiment with the peaceful applications of nuclear energy. There are also visually impressive scenes of massive earth movements resulting from numerous underground explosions. The footage suggests we know more about the effects of nuclear weapons on the environment than on people.

Most other segments fall short of honest documentation, particularly in interviews with representatives from science, government and private industry. And Pettit's caustic comments distract in lieu of inform. He states, "With underground testing there are no fireballs or mushroom clouds to evoke old memories." When Peggy Lee sings "Is That All There Is?" one should ponder, "Why was there so much?" *Footnotes* does not offer a balanced perspective; instead, it fails in attempting to answer objectively the question of whether the bomb should be employed as a peaceful explosive.

18

PHILIP BANDY

"NET Journal":
Hiroshima-Nagasaki

Only hours following the destruction of Hiroshima, a Japanese documentary film unit began recording the effects of the bomb on both the city and its citizens. The result was two hours and forty minutes of unedited film. Japan's documentation of Hiroshima and subsequently Nagasaki was the primary reason the television documentary, *Hiroshima-Nagasaki* was produced by National Educational Television (NET). The NET film was composed of three segments: public reaction to a 1970 photographic exhibit, the condensation of the 1945 Japanese film footage and an edited version of a 1967 BBC documentary. The first segment was concerned with public reaction to a New York Cultural Center photographic exhibit, commemorating the twenty-fifty anniversary of the bombings. The exhibit's audience was an amalgamation of the population and their reaction preserved by skillful, intelligent cinematography. This segment examines how the people reacted when mentally confronted with the realities of nuclear war. Horror and fear in the viewers' faces establish the mood of the remaining film. For example, the documentary reveals the reactions and thoughts of a Japanese student viewing the display. The information was recorded and transferred from the center's guest book onto film. The student wrote: "The photographs brought back to me sharp memories of the day which I shall . . . never be able to forget. . . . Nowdays, it is so peaceful, people cannot be convinced. . . . Only those who went through it know. Even the photographs do not really show the actual horror, the dirt . . . I am glad to be still alive."

The second segment of the documentary comprises the edited Japanese film and was originally produced by Dr. Erik Barnouw; his film is also titled *Hiroshima-Nagasaki—August, 1945*. It depicts on-the-spot filming during the days immediately following the dropping of the atomic bombs (Barnouw's documentary is analyzed later in the text). It should be noted here that United States forces seized all of the original footage during the Occupation; it was immediately classified secret. Twenty-three years elapsed before selected parts of the film were released. Produced by Columbia University's Center for Mass Communications, Barnouw's documentary effectively captures the results of nuclear war.

In his text, *Thermonuclear Warfare*, Paul Anderson warns that those scenes in *Hiroshima-Nagasaki—August, 1945* may reoccur in the future: "Hiroshima-type scenes would be repeated a thousand-fold. . . . How much of this the ordinary survivor, or even the member of a trained cadre like the police, could endure before he himself went into a state of traumatic uselessness, is not known."[1]

The third segment, *The Building of the Bomb*, is taken from a British Broadcasting Company (BBC) documentary. The edited BBC film follows the development of the atomic age through the scientists who made it possible. Yet the film does not focus on the weapon's aftermath but rather on the political pressures exerted to insure the bomb's development.

Chronologically, *The Building of the Bomb* segment should have preceded the Barnouw film. Out of context in this logical sequence, it lost some of its philosophical impact, although its content revealed important information. The documentary presented many of the circumstances leading to the bomb's development, testing and physical aspects. By interviewing prominent scientists who helped develop the weapon, *Building* reflects an immense amount of research. The interviews, though conventional in their approach and content, contained information that was vitally needed to make sound judgments concerning morality and use of the bomb.

Throughout the documentary, both moral issues and atomic destruction were thoroughly examined. Because of the film's structure, however, the main thrust of the documentary was the effect of explosions on the residents of Hiroshima and Nagasaki. The use of and responsibility for the bomb were seldom mentioned. The BBC, for example, did not attempt to pass judgment on the decisions of President Truman; only the issues of the time and the political climate were explicated. In the introduction, the narrator reads excerpts from President Truman's memoirs while still photographs of the remaining rubble of Hiroshima are shown. During certain phases of the reading, a point-counterpoint technique is employed between audio and video. While the narrator reads, "Let there be no mistake, we shall completely destroy Japan's power to make war," scenes of the mutilated bodies of men, women, and children are shown. With another Truman statement, "Atomic energy may, in the future, supplement the power that now comes from coal, oil and falling water," the film editors cut to pictures of crumbled homes—exactly at the point when the narrator intones "falling water." These techniques suggest the producers added editorial comments. These editorial statements are not subtle, but effectively integrated.

In the film, one of the men responsible for collecting the photographs displayed at New York's Cultural Center describes the exhibit's purpose "to focus attention on the nuclear problem as one facing the whole of humanity in which partisan political feelings are irrelevant before the larger issue involved." This statement also applies to the edited section from the BBC documentary. The film strives to change one's attitude toward nuclear war. The horrors projected on slender strips of celluloid are not imaginary. Ignorance of atomic weapons not only breeds fear but prohibits one from making rational nuclear judgments.

If the documentary had been released and shown to the public earlier, doubtless reaction would have been different. In the early fifties, for example, the basic principles of nuclear energy were not widely known and, consequently, the total force and power of atomic weapons could not be imagined. Through ignorance, most people might have discounted the BBC film as an overimaginative Hollywood production or simply as a hoax comparable to the "War of the Worlds" broadcast. Although the events of Hiroshima and Nagasaki were documented, that only one bomb could totally destroy a single city was almost impossible to fathom.

As information concerning atomic energy became more available, the number of viewers who might accept the film as realistic increased. In August 1970, when the NET documentary was televised, there existed sufficient knowledge of the arms race and the workings of nuclear fission. The NET documentary offered additional information to the public, thorough and documented segments from three different areas concerning the possibility of nuclear annihilation. The documentary might easily have been produced in a way that would have offended fewer people; however, the purpose of NET's *Hiroshima-Nagasaki* was to offer information on the development and subsequent results of nuclear warfare and to allow a television audience, in 1970, the opportunity to judge certain facts for themselves. Hopefully, the knowledge of what could happen in a nuclear attack-counterattack might now be sufficient to forestall the possibility of confrontation.

The NET documentary, by examining three areas—the bomb as viewed in the seventies, the destruction of Hiroshima and Nagasaki and the detailed history of the bomb's development—is a major contribution to the documentary genre of nuclear films. Although some manipulation of editing, music, and camera was necessary to subjectively emphasize statements, the film consistently questions the perplexities of human and scientific morality. By focusing on scientists of the 1930s—Oppenheimer, Teller, Serge, Fermi, and Von Heisenberg—the documentary presents a needed historical perspective. It also shows Churchill and Roosevelt as men confronted with ample warnings concerning nuclear weaponry. Finally, the bomb, although initially developed as a defensive weapon, became an offensive weapon. Instead of a deterrent, it opened new paths of knowledge and destruction. The documentary succeeds in characterizing the scientist as humanitarian and the bomb as a weapon too awesome for comprehension.

19

RICHARD TAYLOR

Hiroshima: A Document of the Atomic Bombing

On a warm August afternoon in 1945, Akira Iwasaki and his film crew photographed the ruins of Hiroshima resulting in almost three hours of footage that subsequently remained hidden from public view for twenty-three years. Iwasaki had already been told by the United States to stop filming but they later reconsidered and allowed him to record what is certainly the most accurate and emotional document of man's first use of an atomic device to wage war. Iwasaki's footage remains an important visual record of the bombing. The military, apparently without their own film unit, depended on the Japanese to document the effects of the atom. It seemed unnecessary to dwell on detailed investigations of the destruction. The filmic record of flattened ruins of Hiroshima and Nagasaki provided all the evidence needed. Radiation? It wasn't considered.

The destruction of the two cities provided an end to Japan's earlier goal of a Pacific conquest. To the people of the United States, the bomb had halted the war as suddenly and unexpectedly as Pearl Harbor had started it. To the people of Hiroshima and Nagasaki it started a never-ending sequence of suffering—suffering that would be suppressed for years.

Americans saw only a few carefully selected shots of the leveled cities in national magazines. An illustration of the new-ubiquitous mushroom cloud appeared in *Life* the week the war ended. The bomb's capacity for instant destruction was explained in detail, but its sinister aftereffects were never mentioned. In all fairness, few realized these little-understood effects would soon become the real legacy of horror of the atomic age.

While Hiroshima and Nagasaki still smoldered, the survivors crawled out of the blackened debris. Iwasaki filmed them as they stumbled into the makeshift hospitals crying for help. As the days progressed, he photographed the endless parade of never-healing burns and slow, painful deaths. It was crude photography; the conditions were terrible. The lighting was so diffuse that unknown figures seemed composed against a decaying background; the subject matter is some of the most unappealing footage ever recorded. The American army confiscated the completed film.

Americans slowly learned about the effects of radiation. As more information was released, an alarmed populace began constructing makeshift bomb shelters in their basements and backyards. At the government's request, local civil defense units were formed. Amidst army K rations, children knelt in basement corridors of schools preparing for expected attacks while major cities posted yellow alert signs on their buildings. The nation was plunged deep in the cold war panic. Most information on the effects of nuclear weapons came from the neat, though ambiguous, illustrated civil defense booklets; some slow motion films of dummies at Nevada test sites were also made available on television and in movie theaters. One can only speculate as to the hysteria that might have resulted had the long-forgotten Japanese footage been made available for extensive public viewing. Reading about a possible attack was one thing, seeing it as it actually occurred was another.

In 1968, Professor Erik Barnouw and his staff at the Center of Mass Communications at Columbia University learned of the existence of the Hiroshima-Nagasaki footage. They discovered the Japanese government had been given some film from the National Archives, film that had been classified top secret since World War II. Barnouw and his staff obtained this same footage (only a small part of the original seven thousand feet remained) and used it to assemble a film. The result is *Hiroshima-Nagasaki—August, 1945*, a short, black and white documentary, which apparently uses only the Iwasaki footage.

The opening shots, although never before seen, are now familiar views of the destroyed cities. They are marked by one omission that has remained constant in almost every photograph or film shown of the destruction—there are no people. There is only a desolate, lifeless landscape. Finally, rather suddenly, almost inanimate beings appear. They are burned and twisted figures with skin peeling off, hair coming out in clumps, and babies with melted eyes. It is some of the most authentically horrible footage ever documented. For the first time the actual effects of atomic war are witnessed.

The 1970 Japanese documentary, *Hiroshima: A Document of the Atomic Bombing*, uses some of the same stock footage as Erik Barnouw's *Hiroshima-Nagasaki—August, 1945*. Unlike the Barnouw film, however, *Document* adds a considerable amount of contemporary footage. Scenes of Hiroshima today are contrasted with the rubble of the city of 1945. More important, a sensitive historical treatment of the holocaust's victims is given. Several sequences effectively focus on the survivors of the blast, notably a case history of a woman who was exposed to radiation as a three-year-old child. She died thirty-two years later, from stomach cancer. Director-writer, M. Ogasawa's taut direction blends stills of the victim with motion, giving the impression that although the bomb has gone, its effects remain. His still-motion technique occurs throughout the documentary. Certain scenes, from 1945 through 1970, concentrate on the survivor's constant need for medical attention; their deep psychological wounds, and their inability to fit into everyday life. For the victims, time has stood still since the searing fireball leveled their homes.

Document, however, ignores one of the most heartbreaking aspects of the bomb survivors—most of them were shunned by others. Nonexposed people felt the survivors were unclean and contaminated. Even in 1970 they were known as outcasts, avoided and alone. Although *Document* briefly mentions the tragedy of alienation, it never offers an in-depth exploration.

Nevertheless, *Hiroshima: A Document of the Atomic Bombing* is a visually excellent documentary. Sagacious editing skillfully interweaves past and present, black-and-white stock footage with contemporary color footage, and motion sequences with still shots. Color flash-forwards provide gentle juxtapositions. Color scenes of current memorial services, interspersed with the happy faces of children on tour, are contrasted with Akira Iwasaki's dour and grisly black-and-white scenes of the bomb's immediate aftermath. An impressive lyrical commentary then relates the statistics, explaining that there were no hospital beds, that most of Hiroshima's doctors were killed instantly and 80 percent of the city's nurses were dead.

Ogasawa uses special effects sparingly, adhering to a logical, straightforward treatment which conveys many visual messages relating to the total bomb experience. The compelling imagery is central to Ogasawa's theme. One sequence, for example, explains the fallout's "black rain" by showing black droplets along a wall. A railroad schedule, etched by the fireball, provides a stark reminder of the pervasiveness of the bomb's effects. Ogasawa masterfully arranges other images—crude artwork, slow camera pans of medical records, teacups melted at seven thousand degrees, and human shadows engraved on concrete structures. Melted watches, now placed on antiseptic cotton, reflect the shadows of time standing still.

There are other poignant moments: an injured woman being carried in a child's wagon, the tragedy of the "Hiroshima Maidens," and the story of the paper cranes. Yet each sequence appears as an all-too-brief interlude. Had they been given sufficient consideration, these flashes of imagery would have been more effective.

There is significantly more medical footage in *Document* than in Barnouw's documentary. For example, an autopsy is shown. The camera also focuses on previously withheld medical records, that reveal case histories: a soldier who went insane through delayed effects; a seemingly healthy twelve-year-old girl who suddenly lost her hair and later died.

The strengths of the picture edit are offset by weaknesses in *Document*'s soundtrack. The narration, and to a lesser degree the music, are inappropriate to the mood of the film. These deficiencies may be due to cultural differences or the English translation. Regardless, some major faults are apparent: there are unintended gaps of silence which disrupt the flow. V. Bickley's narration at times does not match the visual action. His delivery is dull and monotone and fails to project the sensitivity of the screenplay.

The music, like the narration, is also fragmented. There are appropriate and ethereal oriental musical segments, but they are haphazardly placed in the soundtrack. One notable exception is the thematic time sequence near the film's beginning. Here, there is a slow zoom-in on a melted pocket watch. The clicking sounds of time and the charred timepiece establish and sustain Ogasawa's theme. The music effectively enhances this key sequence. The narrator poses a rhetorical question: "Is it meaningless to ponder over time that has stopped?" Here, the film production elements work in a harmony of expression.

A great deal of restraint is exercised in *Document*. One problem in showing shock footage is that the numbing effect may take precedence over the message of the film. Such is not the case in *Hiroshima: A Document of the Atomic Bombing*. Authentically horrifying historical scenes are interfaced with the more pleasant and acceptable reality of Hiroshima today. *Document*, in addition to showing stock footage of the atomic holocaust, goes a step further by explaining the human effects.

The film's conclusion, although similar to the final moments of *Hiroshima-Nagasaki—August, 1945*, adds a more eloquent footnote. The narrator explains that a hydrogen bomb of today is twenty-five hundred times as powerful as the Hiroshima bomb. To heighten the impact there are shots of a screaming newborn baby rapidly intercut with aerials of billowing mushroom clouds.

Ogasawa's documentary records, "the hours, days, months and years that followed the bombings." With fearsome appeal to the imagination, it elicits an honest, sympathetic response. It acts as a retrospective testimony to man's inhumanity to man. Through color flash-forwards and a free movement through time, *Document* reveals that life continues for the people of Hiroshima despite the tragedy that occurred in August of 1945.

20

ROBERT W. DUNCAN

Hiroshima-Nagasaki— August, 1945

And on the twentieth day, the silent wasteland of the scorched and leveled city bloomed with exotic plants which had no previous existence on the planet, a brilliant blanket in honor of the thousands whose flesh was blasted into gas by man's finest bomb.

In the makeshift hospitals, men, women, and children, dazed into immobility by pain and the unexpected miracle of instant holocaust, examined their gaping wounds, their peeling flesh, their fused fingers and toes. Others who had been far enough from the central blast to escape such injuries began to falter, retch, and die with a brand new affliction—radiation sickness.

The earliest film record of the bombings of Hiroshima and Nagasaki was kept for twenty-three years at the National Archives in Washington, D.C., first stamped "Secret," then, "Not to be released without approval of the Department of Defense," despite the fact that the film contained no military information. *Hiroshima-Nagasaki—August, 1945*, initially produced by Japanese film makers under the direction of Akira Iwasaki, and later under the supervision of the United States Army, was made available for public viewing through the efforts of Professor Erik Barnouw and his staff, of the Center for Mass Communications at Columbia University. Appalled by the readiness of men in high position to solve problems by mammoth nuclear explosion, Dr. Barnouw felt the interned film might offer some arguments for preventing a repetition of the anguish of Hiroshima and Nagasaki.

The sixteen-minute documentary is all that remains of hours of filming, reduced from the original version. Referring to the eliminated sections, the Defense Department stated, "Out takes from the original production no longer exist, having probably been destroyed during the conversion from acetate to safety film."[1]

The documentary is a film about the ultimate: Death. The voice of Dr. Robert Oppenheimer repeats words from the *Bhagavad-Gita*, the Hindu book of devotion, to describe atomic power: "Now I am become death, the destroyer of worlds."[2] The background music, added by Dr. Barnouw's staff, is an appropriately haunting suggestion of short siren wails. Written by Paul Ronder, and narrated by Ronder and Kazuko Oshima, it is low-key and objective.

The documentary is a remarkably human and historical presentation, primarily because Barnouw had concentrated on creating an accurate view of past holocausts. There are neither subtle nor obvious attempts to overdramatize events; the factual, eloquently stated narration is humane and scientific, maintaining a continuity of thought. Music is used sparingly, the visuals are juxtaposed in a sensitive, compelling manner. The documentary, writes Akira Iwasaki, "is an appeal or warning from man to man for peaceful reflection—to prevent the use of the bomb ever again. . . . It was not the kind of film the Japanese thought Americans would produce."[3]

The film's opening depicts the tranquillity of the "before" scene— quiet roads, buildings, a *torii* gate to a Shinto shrine, crags on a low hill, a crude wooden guard tower manned by sentinels, a soldier looking out under the low roof of a dugout shelter. Then the bomb heaves and climbs to heaven, trembling heavily as it gets its second wind. The mute rubble shows the destruction as astonishingly thorough. A few deformed steel building girders remain at the outer reaches of the solar heart-fire. Tender flowers and vines have left their fragile silhouettes on rocks, fences, and steel beams before evaporating. Further from the center, crippled trees evidence the destructive range of one bomb. A high-steepled church leans dangerously. Bare tortured steel supports are seen through a large shattered window opening as Kazuko Oshima's voice comes softly: "I remember . . . I do not know what has happened . . . I'm searching for a friend." A chalk scrawl on a tottering wall said, "Where are you, sister?" There were women still alive with the floral pattern of their kimonos tattooed on their skin, burned in by the first flash.

Barnouw commented that the editing efforts were difficult because of the "paucity of human-effects footage"; one can only conjecture on what might have been shown had all the footage been made available.

The film has been shown since its release in 1970, most widely at universities and colleges. Made available for ninety-six dollars, five hundred prints were sold in five months. After the commercial networks viewed and rejected it, the documentary was given to National Educational Television (NET). NBC then decided to use it for "First Tuesday," but their offer to "buy out" NET was refused.[4] The immediate demand for this film as soon as it was made available indicates that an audience for such material exists and that it will respond if given the opportunity.

Motion pictures can communicate effectively when even the most eloquent words fail. An early showing of *Hiroshima-Nagasaki—August, 1945*, including the footage irrevocably lost, was not possible. "Why," Barnouw asks, "was this footage declared secret?" "What else," he inquires, "lies silent and sealed in the vaults of the Department of Defense?"

In December 1972, Dale Wile, general manager of NET, in answer to a query for information, related the fate of a sixty-minute documentary ("NET Journal": *Hiroshima-Nagasaki*) which included Barnouw's sixteen-minute film. Legal rights for the NET one-hour production, Wile wrote, "permitted only the single broadcast of the program on August 3, 1970." Other types of uses—closed circuit college screenings and the like—were expressly prohibited. Only the original master of the documentary remains in existence (in vault storage).[5] It is not known why NET chose this hard line or if this position was imposed on them, and if so by whom.

Concerning what some perceive as the threat of censorship, there are a few heartening conclusions from the NET incident. The old cliché about the potential of an individual effort in the face of massed opposition by powerful and intrenched forces takes on fresh significance in view of the results achieved by Dr. Barnouw and his associates, who refused to be dissuaded either by the deliberate institutional inertia or by the sheer volume of investigation and research.

Outside of the commercial agencies, only public television and the university exert their thrust. There are no other facilities that can effectively function on a scale commensurate with the scope of the lavishly financed and staffed commercial media. The most courageous newspapers and magazines have their editorial room "musts," or—as Alexis de Tocqueville might have said—might have a reluctance about offering unwelcome information to a large number of readers who would rather not be disturbed by it.

News film and documentary are the direct descendants of an approach to the texture of actual life which began with the novel, that newest of literary types that arrived with the emergence of a large literate middle class in the seventeenth and eighteenth centuries. While the literature of the aristocracy, the myth and romance, continued, separately as well as fused with the new prose genre, the reading public was increasingly eager to see, hear, and feel what was familiar to daily life. The newspaper's growth paralleled the novel, satisfying the appetite for the real, the true, and the proximate. Hogarth and his lesser contemporaries took the next obvious step with more earthy pictures that, to use Joseph Conrad's well-known statement of artistic purpose, made you *see*. This strain was advanced through the *Illustrated London News*, for example, and photographers like Mathew Brady, while the realistic novels of the nineteenth century and the muckraking movement of the twentieth continued the prose development. The two forms converged in the pictorial essays of *Life, Look*, and other magazines. The financial failure of the two leaders, despite popular success, underlines the need for establishing the film documentary, such as *Hiroshima-Nagasaki—August, 1945*, free of commercial and doctrinaire pressures. It may be simplistic to say a free society deprived of such unrestricted gathering of and access to pictorial documentation is endangered, but it is tempting to assert it.

The Atom Strikes, available from United States Army Films, makes a provocative companion piece to *Hiroshima-Nagasaki—August, 1945*. Its thirty-one-minute survey covers the early New Mexico blast and the bombings of Hiroshima and Nagasaki. The footage shows no burned or maimed human beings; the scenes are devoted only to the examination of objects such as twisted steel buildings, a commercial museum, and a Russian-Japanese war memorial. Occasionally, Japanese citizens are seen off in the distance; they seem to be healthy and whole pedestrians and cyclists. From these scenes, unlike Barnouw's documentary, there is the strong presumption that the film was not made by the army immediately after the disaster, but months later.

The narration in *Strikes* focuses on technical data, explaining the bomb was programmed to explode at a higher altitude to "reduce radio-active dissipation." As evidences of damage appear (while an

American soldier points at selected objects), the narrator explains "the shadows of posts etched on the floor of a bridge, the shadow of a pedestrian," which, says the narrator, "tells its own meaningful story." A damaged Red Cross hospital is seen with walls blown in, or out, but without a person in sight except the guide. The narrator also states the hospital never ceased operating.

The Atom Strikes suggests that at that time the use of the bombs over Japan was morally acceptable, that radiation did not cause civilians to suffer. These viewpoints become evident when a priest at a Jesuit seminary, located four miles from the detonation core, is interviewed by the army. His composure would seem to indicate it had been some time since the bombing; he spoke as objectively as if he had been lecturing a class. He said he saw the wounded, their burns, "especially parts of the body not covered by clothing." There were no facilities for treating the injured (an apparent contradiction as the narrator earlier stated the Red Cross hospital "never ceased operating"). In response to other questions, he states that nobody was available to take charge because most of the important people had been killed; there were no ill effects from radiation among those who worked with the wounded and in the ruins after the blast; and he had not heard a single outburst of hate toward the United States. On the whole, the remaining Japanese expressed admiration for American technical skill.

He concluded with a statement of some length on the difficulty of making a moral judgment on the bombing. His position was that war itself is the basic moral challenge and must be evaluated before we can make an assertion about the atom bomb's threat to civilians. In the final fade-out, accompanied by a heavy, dramatic musical score, the narrator said: "This is the record. Endless man-hours of work. Two B-29's, two bombs, two cities. The tabulation of the record speaks for itself."

The Atom Strikes focuses on the destruction of objects while *Hiroshima-Nagasaki—August, 1945* depicts actual human suffering—the voice of Kazuko Oshima, in Barnouw's film, explains: "People look awful . . . skin comes off . . . if I'm in hell it is like this."

Another United States Army film, *A Tale of Two Cities*, contains much of the same footage as *The Atom Strikes*. The running time, however, is only twelve minutes and there are some interesting modifications. The narration is different—the rhetoric and the delivery are more persuasive and professional. The seriously damaged Red Cross hospital was shown, but there was no accompanying assertion that the hospital did not cease operation. Although the interview with the priest was included, there were important omissions. Of the three questions posed in *The Atom Strikes*, concerning the dangers of radiation among Japanese workers, the priest is seen responding to only one. More significant, perhaps, is the complete deletion of his prepared statement on the lack of Japan's hostility toward the United States.

These films, although possessing different views, are remarkable first steps in helping to understand the meaning of nuclear war. They offer important documentation and merit extensive distribution not only at universities but on both commercial and public television.

21

JAMES HALL AND
JACK G. SHAHEEN

To Die, To Live

To Die, To Live is a special nuclear genre documentary. It is the only film to carefully examine psychological responses of Hiroshima survivors. Based on Dr. Robert Jay Lifton's pioneering study, *Death in Life: Survivors of Hiroshima*, it conveys a sympathetic view of the profound and enduring mental images associated with A-bomb exposure.

The documentary was drawn from Lifton's original 1962 interviews with A-bomb survivors (*hibakusha*, as they are referred to in both text and film). It was directed and written by a Hungarian concentration camp survivor, Robert Vas. Impressed with Lifton's book, Vas met with him to discuss how to best approach the subject and the feasibility of reinterviewing Hiroshima survivors. Subsequently, *To Die, To Live* was commissioned by the British and Canadian Broadcasting Corporations.

In order to supplement the documentary's central purpose, Vas needed vivid and authentic film images. He spent two weeks in the National Archives in Washington, D.C., searching for appropriate stock footage of the Hiroshima-Nagasaki bombings. Some of the footage had recently been declassified. The stock footage and still photographs, intermingled with contemporary scenes of Hiroshima form the essence of *To Die, To Live*. The film constantly moves back and forth between Hiroshima, 1975, and the time of the bomb.

The purpose of the film is to document survivors' reactions to the A-bomb and to evoke a better understanding of their experience. More important than a formal statement of purpose are the combined objectives of Lifton and Vas. As researcher and interpreter, they evoke the quality of the holocaust in a sensitive and meaningful manner. The imagery of the book is artistically transferred to the film: "It would have been wrong for [Vas] to duplicate the book on film—he couldn't do that. . . . The filmmaker has to, in a way, recreate the event in his own fashion and deviate radically from the book in order to make a good film. . . . One cannot focus on just the book and claim that [the film] must follow those criteria. The book must be the inspiration for the film, and the film must have some of the basic sensibility of the book, . . . but it has to make its own statement." [1]

The ultimate success of the documentary lies not only in fulfilling objectives but in the broader area of supplementing knowledge and creating new dimensions of awareness. *To Die, To Live*, however, is not entirely successful. There are some obvious weaknesses. Exceedingly lengthy moments of imagery tend to distract from the film's purpose. The attention given to certain scenes lingers; at times the survivors' plight is overstated. Vas presents the survivor experience in five unified sections. Each section concludes by introducing the next sequence. A title card stating the section's theme then appears. Here, the technique becomes confusing, breaking rather than enhancing continuity. It is difficult to discern where one section concludes and the other begins. The employment of title cards slows the film's progression. The words are improperly framed and difficult to read. Thus, the transitions between sequences provide an unnatural disruption in the flow of the documentary.

To Die, To Live begins with contemporary footage reflecting a typical day. The sun rises over Japan's inland sea, haunting music builds in the background. The action shifts to a cross-section of early morning Hiroshima life: shops opening, sparse traffic, schoolchildren leaving for classes, fishermen embarking, and the face of a clock indicating the passage of time. Integrated into these scenes is the black-and-white 1945 newsreel footage of the A-bomb wounded. Those afflicted of the past and those nonafflicted of the present offer stark visual contrasts between normal life and life after the bomb. This technique is effectively employed throughout the film.

Time continues to pass in modern Hiroshima. A hilltop view of a bridge is shown. The camera cuts to water shimmering in a gentle, hypnotic rhythm. Highlights reflect brilliantly. Relating his encounter with the bomb, a survivor notes: "The sky was serene, the air was flooded with glittering morning light. My steps were slow along the dry, dusty road. . . . The sirens . . . had just given the all-clear signal. I had reached the foot of a bridge where I halted, and was turning my eyes toward the water." The screen goes black; the narration continues: "A blinding . . . flash cut sharply across the sky. . . . I threw myself onto the ground. . . . At the same moment as the flash, the skin over my body felt a burning heat. . . . [Then there was] a blank in time . . . dead silence . . . probably a few seconds . . . and then a . . . huge 'boom.'" For the survivor, time stands still. The course of history becomes irreversible.

The camera occasionally cuts to artwork depicting the bomb. Stills of the dead are shown. A title reads: "A sudden shift from normal existence to an overwhelming and lifelong encounter with death." Other images, both visual and auditory, emphasize the apocryphal finality of the experience. Stock footage shows a dog scavenging through the destruction. A montage of stills reveals blackened and burned bodies.

Interweaving the present and past, a fundamental appreciation for the unanticipated apocalypse and its all-pervasive death symbol is conveyed. Shadows of Hiroshima citizens (contemporary footage) are juxtaposed against the permanence of those shadows created by the bomb's flash (stock footage).

An almost undetectable transition leads the viewer into the second segment. A woman's voice is heard: "There is one thing that still burdens my conscience. . . . While escaping, I heard a father's cry . . . help! help! . . . If only I had held out a helping hand." A title appears: "Death Guilt." A man poignantly relates an intense image of a charred baby in verse. A former soldier, recalling his inability to offer a dying child water, founded an orphanage. Each day he visits a shrine and makes a symbolic offering of water. Though Vas's intended effect was to convey a sense of overwhelming guilt, the action appears contrived. The sequence points attention to itself because the symbolism, instead of being natural or subtle, is obvious and stilted.

Stock footage introduces the third segment. The narrator intones: "At the end of two weeks, which was the critical period, burns and cuts which appeared to be curing, suddenly worsened." Again, a title appears: "Invisible Contamination—the image of a weapon that leaves behind deadly influences which may strike at any time."

Hibakusha relate their self-perpetuating fears of "A-bomb disease": "We heard the new phrase. 'A-bomb disease.' The fear in us became strong, especially when we would see certain things with our eyes: a man looking perfectly well as he rode by on a bicycle one morning, suddenly vomiting blood, and then dying. . . . Soon we were all worried about our health, about our own bodies—whether we would live or die." The unpredictable effects of irradiation and exposure are intertwined with visuals of a new Hiroshima. Modern shopping scenes are interwoven with the reconstruction. The sequence suggests people continue to die even as Hiroshima rebuilds and regains vitality. A-bomb hospital patients are portrayed as biding time by watching television; an instant soup commercial espouses health and smiles in stark contrast to the abundant infirmity and despair (the death vigil) in the hospital.

Protective parents fret over possible symptoms appearing in their children and contemplate genetic damage occurring in future generations. "I don't want my children to increase our family," says a mother, "I'm very much afraid."

The fourth part of *To Die, To Live* is concerned with segregation and discrimination by and against Hiroshima's survivors. Wails of ceremonial whistles, resembling the haunting sound of a saxophone, introduce a wedding ceremony. As the ceremony proceeds, a middle-aged woman speaks. Inner turmoil registers on her scarred face as she recounts: "Like everyone else, I had a dream . . . I fell in love with a man and wanted to marry him . . . but when I got these burn-scars all over my body, I had to give up that dream. . . . My fiancé came to visit me at the hospital. I didn't want him to see me as I was so I covered myself from top to bottom with my kimono." The ceremony continues as her voice interchanges with the translation. The camera then cuts to a photograph of a disfigured woman, perhaps the one who is speaking. Simultaneously, as the ceremony reaches its climax, she concludes bitterly, "Then I broke off the engagement."

Relating his feelings about the most obvious *hibakusha* stigmata, a Hiroshima resident explains: "Of all the things connected with those days, what makes the strongest impression on me is the mark of a burn-scar . . . the keloid . . . I really hate to see a keloid. . . . Even if I try to forget about the bomb, I cannot. We see such people here all of the time and unless these people disappear, I will be unable to forget." A title reads: "*Hibakusha*—'A-bomb outcast'—'A-bomb man.'"

The camera unrelentingly concentrates on the keloids in stock footage and current interviews. The scenes seem as one: an uncomfortable reality is graphically depicted. One is able to look beyond the keloid. The scenes assist the receptive viewer in overcoming superficial revulsion. Survivors are seen as being victimized because they are victims: "In employment and marriage . . . *hibakusha* are treated with discrimination. . . . [They are considered somehow] inferior. [There is no] fundamental appreciation for the fact these people were physically affected by the greatest force . . . unprecedented in history."

The final segment of the documentary is a general statement relating the events of 1945 to 1975. It begins with shots of the Peace Park, Hiroshima's memorial to the legacy of the bomb. An elderly gentleman plays a single-string traditional instrument while sitting on a park bench. As people stroll through the park and children play, the desolate rasping of the instrument is heard. The scene pervades a reflective mood: "To remember—To forget—To bear witness."

Recollection is developed first, by a visit to the atomic museum, and second, by an examination of the art of calligraphy. In the atomic museum, a multilingual audio guide directs people through the exhibits. In each display, the effects of the fireball are depersonalized—from effects on articles of clothing to beer bottles. Tape-recorded voices advise museum patrons, "When you have finished your observation, please move on." As the narration fades, the action shifts to views of a river; bridges and muddy water are shown.

Water is a recurring theme. Each section reveals cinematic expressions of shifting water colors: gray, blue, purple, and black. Vas seldom moves the camera; he simply permits the water to remain motionless, suggesting the indelible mark of the water on the survivors. This is demonstrated by a family man's struggle to forget. In 1962, he said: "On the way here . . . I saw children swimming in the river. Those who went through the bomb would never swim there. . . . I remember passing that spot and seeing dead bodies floating on the water." In May of 1975, he noted: "My feelings have changed. I take my children to the Peace Park. In the park we play together and play with the pigeons. I feel everything is alright now. I'm healthy and so is my family . . . we forget . . . things change." The scene also reveals that he now accepts the river—he takes his children rowing.

Conflicting opinions about Hiroshima's "city of peace" image are offered. The bearing witness sequence focuses on contemporary scenes of the August 6 commemoration. A survivor relates his special feelings: "When the day comes around . . . the memory of the bomb comes back to me. . . . I have the feeling that I must go there [to the Peace Park]. . . . If I don't go, I have the feeling something is wrong—I go there because I want to sleep peacefully."

In contrast, a history professor relates his distaste. The narration is developed visually by shots of camera-toting tourists, sight-seeing busses, postcards of the ruins and other souvenir trade: "Around August sixth, they hold all kinds of noisy festivals. . . . I used to have to get out of the city because I found it unbearable . . . I felt like slapping people for doing this. . . . Take the Atomic Dome . . . it has become a sightseeing object. . . . Thirty years ago, the river near the dome was full of corpses . . . I don't see why we keep up the dome . . . it isn't the actual spot where the bomb fell. At that spot, there should be nothing . . . they should leave the land bare . . . nothingness."

At this point, the film reaches a natural and forceful conclusion. Screen action, however, continues. Dusk sets over the city. As an evening baseball game progresses, the Atomic Dome is silhouetted in the background. The dome's outline against the final reddish rays of the sun on the horizon has an ethereal quality. Hiroshima night life is observed: entertainment clubs, neon-lit street scenes, and a striptease act performed to the slow-tempo accompaniment of, "Where Do I Begin?" Church organ music is cross-faded. Stock film shows four *hibakusha* raising their burned arms; another four victims attempt a clenched fist with their damaged hands; one man, in spite of heavy keloids about the mouth, goes through the motions of speaking. The screen fades to black, the organ music trails off, and the film abruptly concludes.

The ending is not satisfying. It is esoteric, lacking the finality of an effective documentary conclusion. The sequences, beginning with the baseball game and concluding with stock footage of the *hibakusha* are vague footnotes. They fail to meaningfully summarize Lifton's theme.

The conclusion is out of context when compared with the rest of the film, for it tends to minimize the effects, which have been previously emphasized. A more suitable ending would have been the survivor's message about the commemoration of August 6: "If we commemorate that day . . . all doors in Hiroshima [should be] closed. . . . People would say, 'I went to Hiroshima on August sixth and all doors were closed. Hiroshima was a city of the dead.'"

The mood of *To Die, To Live* is fundamentally restrained. Several factors contribute to its understated quality. Cinematography in the con-

temporary footage reflects esthetic restraint. The action depicted is subdued, the pace proceeds slowly and deliberately. A consistent gray cast
is maintained; bright sunlight is generally avoided. The colors are
muted. Soft focus and gentle contrasts contribute to the visual mood.
The gaiety of a rooftop amusement park is offset by a threatening,
cloudy sky; bashful schoolgirls are silently aware of the camera's
presence, flatly lit by skyscraper-shadowed sunlight. The use of stills,
sometimes almost indistinguishable from stock footage, is effective in
maintaining an unobtrusive level of activity. An almost-equal propor-
tion of stock-still footage to contemporary footage allows no single
image or technique to dominate.

The use of sound conveys a proper, soothing mood. The narration,
with the exception of Vas's three explanatory statements and original
sound from stock film soundtracks, is composed entirely of the *hiba-
kushas'* own words. There are periods of complete silence and a wide
variety of musical themes employed. Vas's musical articulateness becomes evident in the soundtrack. Many different musical forms are
represented within the rare occasions in which music is used: "Also
Sprach Zarathustra" (the theme from *2001: A Space Odyssey*) accompanies a segment of stock footage, an elderly man plays a traditional
instrument in the Peace Park. Shrill whistles comprise part of a wedding
ceremony, a striptease act is performed with a piano background,
romantic ballads are played on a background music system in a shopping mall, and church organ music develops the final sequence. The
range of music is generally inconspicuous, blending well with the com-
posite message.

Vas chose the most vivid and important *hibakusha* responses to develop each sequence. Four narrators offer a reserved tone, emotion is
transmitted through pauses. With the on-camera interviews, the survivors' facial expressions punctuate the narration. In order to convey
additional increments of expression, their voices are sometimes retained
on the soundtrack. As the film progresses, the voices of the narrators
become indistinguishable. The experiences of all survivors become one
—the A-bomb is a collective experience to those who survived.

The purposes of author and documentarist diverge. The type of carefully detailed study employed in the book would offer an overkill of
technical facts to the documentary viewer. Because the film's intention
was to convey the basic impression of Lifton's book, the method and
treatment addressed unique criteria. Lifton explains: "The film con-

stantly struggles between what you might call documentary information and artistic evocation. As a documentary impulse, we wanted [to convey] information about what the bomb did. On the other hand, as a creative filmmaker, [Director Vas] wanted to evoke the experience in some artistic way. The film struggles with those two efforts. . . . and sometimes succeeds in blending them."[2] The optimum condition for success falls somewhere between an abundance of symbolic expression and pure data. *To Die, To Live* offers a proper balance. Director Vas's interpretation of the subject matter, in spite of the inconclusive ending, achieves its purpose—Hiroshima, 1975, and Hiroshima, 1945, are a single entity.

Critic John Leonard of the *New York Times*, however, thought *To Die, To Live* contained crude juxtapositions of "disfigured women and department store mannequins." Leonard contended his emotions were being improperly manipulated. He rejected the film's thesis, noting: "[It] was a stomach-turning program. . . . I didn't want to watch a whole hour of it. . . . I thought the subtleties . . . were obscured by a piling-on of images intended, and guaranteed, to shock. Mutilated bodies look the same, don't they, at death camps and at Dresden and at train wrecks? What, in this wretched century is so special about Hiroshima."[3]

Leonard's comments notwithstanding, *To Die, To Live* is an excellent documentary with a strong statement about the bomb's effect on people. The film may occasionally be perceived as brutal on the gut-reaction level, but it is actually intellectually brutal. It reveals something about our world we would rather not see. It relates a reality we do not wish to experience. As Lifton noted prior to its American screening, "Again I was reminded that Hiroshima is not the world's past, but possibly its future."[4]

22 JODY STONE

Rumours of War

Time has dulled the memories of Hiroshima and Nagasaki. Today, Americans rake leaves, exposing their lawns to a few more days of Indian summer, refusing to acknowledge the horrors did not end, but began, in 1945. The continuing reality of the nuclear arms race is presented in chilling, low-key form in the British Broadcasting Corporation's documentary, *Rumours of War*.

Color shots of neatly trimmed lawns and comfortable houses in Albuquerque are contrasted with stark, black-and-white still frames of Hiroshima—people blindly participating in a nuclear arms buildup spliced between the blinding atomic nightmare. Narrator Paul Vaughan's almost monotone voice reveals a frightening nightmare; he sounds like an aloof doctor informing a patient he has terminal cancer. Perhaps the style of narration is intentional; the nuclear arms race resembles a cancer that may eventually erode mankind. The disease continues without an apparent cure.

Rumours opens with a middle-aged weekend gardener; he is not unlike most children of the nuclear age, except that he goes to work every morning at an Albuquerque missile base. His job is to destroy mankind, if necessary, on orders from a "preprogrammed president." The film concentrates on revealing the gardener's restlessness. Narrator Vaughan says the major problem facing the missile base engineers is boredom. The gardener, like most nuclear age victims, has accepted this fact; during his daily routine he thinks little about his ultimate task. Captain Markinson, the gentle leaf-raker, may one day "take part in the destruction of whole nations and ultimately himself and his family." He and his coworkers regularly undergo psychiatric tests.

They work in teams, one man observes the other; both carry pistols. If one suffers a psychological breakdown, the other must shoot him. One point the documentary fails to explain is what the consequences might be if the berserk man shoots first. Although the film does suggest it is unlikely a mistaken launching could occur unless four men in two separate control areas lost their reason simultaneously, it does not successfully answer the shooting dilemma. With the burden of mankind on one's shoulders every day for many years, there is no guarantee that even the most insensitive, thoroughly tested men could remain sane. Another factor overlooked by *Rumours* is the possibility of an irresponsible president or sabotage by a base scientist. Instead, to heighten anxiety, the narrator informs us that six missiles have failed in selective tests, and a Minuteman can never be recalled once it is launched.

The film's pace is as slow as the narration is low-key. Cinematically, the composition is often dull and repetitive. One grows weary, awaiting relief from the continual bombardment of facts and figures. The viewer is nearly able to comprehend Captain Markinson's boredom from repeating routine drills.

Writer-producer Peter Jones, however, reawakens our senses with impressive data: sprints can be fired at twelve thousand miles per hour; "accidents" occur once every ten years, creating the danger of a nuclear blast above an American city. MIRVs, needle-shaped missiles with long, flared tails, may enter the atmosphere without being detected. Seconds after one explodes above one city, others explode at other targets. Radar is virtually defenseless against today's complex missile systems. Decoys, fragments from exploding space busses and pencil-shaped missiles create confusion for an enemy. The enemy also could confuse us. Single warheads are being replaced with multiple warheads, tripling the potency of land-based missiles and increasing by ten-fold the firepower of nuclear arms launched from submarines. Scientist Dr. Edward York says: "It's impossible to win the arms race."

There are a few moments of relief, all conveying the blackest of humor. An animated section dramatically displays the apparent futility of arms limitations negotiations. If the Russians call for a halt to plutonium production, it would be because the United States has an abundant supply. If the Americans call for scrapping medium-ranged bombers, no doubt the fact that it would eliminate 80 percent of the Soviet force had something to do with it. Even on points of agreement, notes

Dr. York, the accord has little real significance. Although both super-powers agreed to test only underground, the film labels the plan as merely an "antipollution device," noting that testing not only continued, but increased.

On occasion, there are cutaways to subjective caricatures in an attempt to ease the shock of the nuclear nightmare. In one animated sketch, a nondescript but obviously horrified man is strapped to a giant projectile loaded with TNT. There has been enough nuclear firepower developed since 1963 to supply a blast equal to a minimum of ten tons of TNT per person. The sketch casually suggests there is no stronger verb than overkill.

The ultimate tragedy of the nuclear age would be other Hiroshimas. But there are daily tragedies, subtle personal ones, born of a mammoth industry that thrives on the arms race. *Rumours* delves, though somewhat superficially, into the lives of sensitive, peace-loving men whose livelihood is derived from building nuclear weapons. Arthur Overmayer, like Captain Markinson, lives in a cozy suburban home, complete with frolicking children greeting him as he walks through a neatly manicured lawn. Overmayer's scientific career began after he had discovered nuclear effects on plastic. However, Overmayer felt "swallowed up by the military-industrial complex; manipulated by remote bureaucratic machines." He became politically active, helping to elect a peace-loving priest to Congress. A question unanswered is Overmayer's motives behind campaigning against the military-industrial complex. Why is he trying to slay the giant that feeds his family? Obviously a sensitive man, Overmayer is well aware that man may be doomed if the nuclear arms buildup continues. However, an abrupt production halt would force him to lose the trappings that come with the good life.

The children of the nuclear age learn their lessons well. One of the most interesting segments of *Rumours* traces a tour of the Sandia Atomic Museum in Albuquerque, New Mexico by a group of Boy Scouts. The museum is filled with nuclear memorabilia; on display are thirty-eight nuclear bombs, thirty scale models, twelve charts on A-bomb history, and a copy of the warning leaflet that was never dropped over Japan. The youngsters, who have lived their entire lives in the shadows of Hiroshima and Nagasaki, are dutifully told by their scoutmaster that "a free world should maintain a deterrent against aggression." The scouts are led to replicas of the weapons used to take the lives of hundreds of thousands. The curator, pleased with the display, states "Things are moving so fast, . . . they will soon be like bows and arrows. Without this museum, future generations wouldn't know what these things looked like." The bomb that annihilated Nagasaki is called "Little Boy." The bomb that brought hell on earth to Hiroshima is "Fat Man." Perpetuating fairy tales, the guide insinuates that an object called "Little Boy" certainly could not be evil, leaving only one conclusion for the children to draw. The opponents, victims if you wish, of "Little Boy" must then be evil.

A scout parrots the clichés of his elders: "There's meant to be wars. It's unpleasant, but there's meant to be wars." The scout leader clarifies, "That's the boy's religious training coming out. . . . In the Bible, it says that there will be wars and rumours of wars."

Perhaps T. S. Eliot was right when he stated, more than two decades ago, "This is the way the world ends/Not with a bang but a whimper." Yet the world did not terminate in 1945, nor is it likely that civilization will meet its end in a glorious detonation of nuclear bombs. The nuclear cancer is exemplified by sensitive men doing insensitive jobs and beautiful children parroting ugly dogma. The cold war paranoia has been infiltrating the core of civilization for more than a quarter of a century. As *Rumours* says, the real horror is not the bomb itself, but constant anxiety. Fear comes partly from horror stories of unstoppable missiles; nuclear war is "like firing bullets at bullets." Fear comes partly from a vague notion that civilization could end in a matter of moments. Fear comes from the futility felt by nondecision makers, who idly watch while powerful nations stockpile nuclear arms. Man cannot face the constant fear of a nuclear age without being affected. Most people emulate Captain Markinson's wife; she ignores a problem too enormous to face, saying, "I'd rather not think about it at all."

According to *Rumours*, India, Japan, Italy, Sweden, Israel, Argentina, Austria, Belgium, Canada, The Netherlands, West Germany, and Switzerland will soon have nuclear capabilities. (Since the film was produced, India and Israel have developed atomic bombs.) Social unrest is also blamed on the missile race. Jerome Wisener of Massachusetts Institute of Technology comments that unless the superpowers manage to check one another in a huge, global chess match, the quality of life will deteriorate.

Rumours is an excellent film, suggesting the anxiety of life today is the unexpected, unwanted fallout of a cold war and nuclear stockpiling.

Focusing on areas such as the present size of arsenals, small nation accessibility to weapons, and humanistic problems facing dedicated men, the documentary thoroughly depicts the crucial need for an immediate curtailment of the nuclear arms race.

The interpretive function of *Rumours* is expressed creatively; it conveys more than actual information. The film accurately observes the form and meaning of a specific problem by directing its attention on those individuals responsible for maintaining the nation's stockpile of arms. The human element is explored not through sensationalism or with the aid of an overdramatic musical score but rather by concentrating on most aspects of human behavior—from the raking of leaves to the routine drills at the missile base. The relationship of man to his family, work, and society is a graphic analysis which suggests the nuclear problem is not technical, but one which requires man's exploration and psychological understanding.

23 GEORGE A. MASTROIANNI

Arms and Security:
How Much Is Enough?

The point of view explicated in the ABC documentary, *Arms and Security: How Much Is Enough?*, is that modern technological advances have made the concept of nuclear war increasingly alarming. Nearly a decade after *Dr. Strangelove, Fail Safe*, and other feature films, it reminds us that the bomb has not disappeared. Written and produced by James Benjamin and directed by Howard Enders, the film thoroughly examines the arms race between the United States and the Soviet Union, the surrounding issues and efforts to curtail the escalation.

Arms and Security reconstructs past events in a logical framework. Proposals for controlling atomic energy date back to 1946, Bernard Baruch's Proposal, the Soviet response, and the Andrei Gromyko Plan. Both disarmament proposals, considered unrealistic, were rejected. Subsequently, the nuclear arms race began with the United States moving quickly to outdistance the Soviets.[1] Since the forties both countries have seesawed on a nuclear playground, trying to stay even with each other. Eventually, disarmament hopes gave way to nuclear weapons control and limitation with the Test Ban Treaty, the Sea Bed Treaty, and, in 1972, the Anti-Ballistic Missile (ABM) Treaty, and an interim agreement on Strategic Offensive Weapons.

Arms and Security notes the ABM Treaty permits two anti-ballistic missile defense sites for each nation—one to protect the national capital and the other to protect enough ICBM's for a second-strike capability. The Offensive Weapons Agreement establishes a five-year freeze on ICBMs, with the United States limited to 1,054 missiles and Russia to 1,618. This same agreement limits the United States to 710 submarine-launched missiles and the Soviet Union to 950.

Arms and Security does more than reveal a compilation of significant facts and figures. It is not a documentation of horror, showing nuclear war and its aftermath. Rather, it is a documentary possessing objectivity with reason.

One of the more effective scenes occurs in the underground silos where 150 Minuteman ICBMs are poised. Sixty-five feet below the ground in a Launch Control Capsule, reporter Jules Bergman and his camera crew are locked in behind a four-foot thick, four-ton heavy door. Two Strategic Air Command officers go through a drill, simulating actual launch procedures. The triggering keys are intentionally located on opposite sides of the room for added security, and both must be turned within two seconds of each other. A captain tells Bergman that two keys alone are not enough to launch the missiles. Another capsule control center and two other men turning another pair of keys is a "second vote" to launch 50 Minuteman missiles. Each missile contains hydrogen warheads whose explosive power equals a million tons of TNT. Each is independently programmed for a specific target in the Soviet Union, perhaps an area known to have silos holding the SS-9, the Soviet ICBM.

Reporter Bergman asks, "Could yours and another launch capsule launch a series of missiles without any approval from anybody higher up?" A youthful lieutenant responds, "Yes, uh, they could, but that's why the system was built this way and why we are continually watched." The lieutenant continues, "The probability of having four people, which is what it would take—four different officers and two different capsules—to launch these missiles is very small." The captain adds, "I think there is a lot of personal integrity involved in this type of job. Especially when you're down here with the door locked, nobody can see in and it's up to the individual what he makes of it." Later in the program, a close-up of the lieutenant covers the screen. He says: "If we ever have to turn the keys, we have failed. It's also the system that has failed and the world that has failed if the key turn ever has to come." Bergman's interviews are meaningful because the officers honestly react to carefully selected questions.

As its three main issues, the documentary presents the primary topics that occur during most discussions of nuclear armaments. The film analyzes essential questions: Is a continuing buildup a sane method of defense? Is the price tag too high? Is man inherently warlike? Concerning defense, the director of Research and Development in the U.S. Department of Defense, Dr. John S. Foster, tells reporter Frank Reynolds that he believes this country is safe from enemy attack. Our nuclear-equipped missiles are numerous and powerful enough to destroy most major Soviet cities thirty-four times over, he assures us. Conversely, our major cities can be wiped out by the Russians only thirteen times. Our defensive systems are sophisticated enough to detect a Russian missile launch thirty seconds after it leaves its silo. Satellite and seismograph surveillances allow us to monitor USSR weapons development with a high degree of accuracy.

Although former United States Senator J. William Fulbright and Senator Jacob Javits agree on our defensive capabilities, they feel it is time to end the nuclear arms race—each nation has sufficient power to destroy the other several times over. Thus they contend taxpayers should not support further weapon expenditures.

Despite evidence of our security, some believe we are trailing the Russians. *Arms and Security* focuses on the American Security Council, a private organization with 135,000 individual and 1,500 financial supporters; the organization campaigns against establishing disarmament agreements with Russia. Members of the group also attend seminars called the "cold war college," whose curriculum details the rise of Russian military excellence and the waning of America's superiority. Dr. Herbert York, a member of this group, is a former director of Research and Development in the Department of Defense. York believes that any American insecurity is related to "overkill." There is less security today, he contends, because the arms race of the past twenty years has increased the destructive power of weapons systems to increase the loss of life and property that could result in a nuclear war. Dr. Edward Teller, "the father of the H-bomb," responded to York's "overkill" theory. His comments are actually an excerpt from a film, *Only the Strong*, sponsored by the American Security Council—

> Let me tell you, I don't think the Russians will strike us first, but they may, and they may blackmail us, and the result may be that there will be no America left. We are not prepared. If the Russians attack us, much more than half our people will be killed. America will cease to exist as a power, perhaps even as a memory. . . . They have a plan for civil

defense. If they carry out that plan, then even if our retaliation succeeds, even if we destroy their cities and I don't know that we can, they will have fewer losses of human life than the Second World War, and they will have all the world as their slaves to rebuild their cities.[2]

Protection from a Soviet enslavement as envisioned by Teller is an expensive undertaking. In *Arms and Security*, he explains the first 750 F-15 fighters would each cost $10.5 million. To reduce the price, $6 million per plane, the F-15s would have to be constructed by the thousands. According to economist John Kenneth Galbraith, cost overrun is a problem arising from large, government-supported industries. In the film, Galbraith contends these industries are "quasi-branches of the bureaucracy, extensions of the Pentagon." Constant waste results, adds Galbraith, because new weapons render others obsolete. Thus, competition in developing weapons systems necessitates higher defense costs to counteract more sophisticated developments. Features not needed are built into weapons. Apparently, "nothing too good for the American fighting man" is a costly philosophy.

Former Defense Secretary Melvin Laird explained to Frank Reynolds that reductions in spending are only possible with new treaties. Until then, development must continue. This hard line has been American nuclear policy. Galbraith counters those who believe that a continuing nuclear buildup is an integral part of a healthy American economy, "We just can't bring ourselves to the kind of obscene solution of our economic troubles which requires us to spend for military purposes." He suggests more arms limitations talks to curb spending.

Arms and Security continues to offer added insights into the complexities of the nuclear race. Dr. Richard Barnet notes that military spending can be reduced "without massive economic dislocations, if, in fact, the government is prepared to invest in the economy on such a scale and in such a way as to attract the people in this country to make use of our tremendous productive energy." Barnet recommends our energies be redirected to rebuilding cities and cleaning up the environment. Dr. Jerome Frank, professor of psychiatry at Johns Hopkins University School of Medicine, claims war is not inevitable. He offers a reasonable solution of arms and security problems: "I think we can say today the conditions of life that made war useful are disappearing and the same result should take place if we don't destroy ourselves before we understand what has happened." Describing the delicate international act of balancing the bomb, he says, "In today's world . . . in a nuclear war no one wins—the ground rules are changed. Therefore, we must cooperate with those who are equally as strong in order to survive." Narrator Frank Reynolds poses another view: "Those who have studied aggression in animals have determined that the rare species that kill their own, out of aggressive urges, are the rat family . . . and the family of man."

Perhaps one major asset of ABC's documentary is its timeliness. *Arms and Security* was broadcast 7 August 1972, three days after the Senate overwhelmingly (88–2) approved the ABM treaty, which was slightly delayed because of reservations from United States Senator Henry Jackson. He believed that numerical equality of missiles was essential in a final agreement and wanted Congress to agree.[3] On September 14, approximately five weeks following the broadcast, the Senate gave final approval to the Offensive Arms Agreement, as amended by Jackson. The agreement was subsequently passed by the House of Representatives and signed by President Richard M. Nixon. Both the interim agreement and the ABM treaty went into effect 3 October 1972.

This needed sense of timeliness, supported by balanced interviews and a literate script, serves to strengthen the viewer's perceptions of the nuclear arms race.

The impact of this documentary is also due to its cinematic qualities. Its structure, facts, issues, ideas, and emotional content are enhanced by a dynamic visual style. Throughout the film, writer-producer James Benjamin was able to maintain interest by avoiding lengthy interview segments of people talking directly into the camera's lens. Filmed interviews were employed to discuss issues, and whenever feasible, Benjamin instructed director Howard Enders to use film as a visual backdrop. Nowhere is this more vividly depicted than in the final act. The topic was man's inherent nature, whether he is biologically warlike. Narrator Reynolds is off-camera describing a reenactment of the first battle of the American Revolution. Benjamin then moves to an interview between Reynolds and Dr. Jerome Frank. During sections of the interview there are cuts back and forth between the Lexington-Concord reenactment. Here, Benjamin creates a visual expression of the glorification of war as it relates to Americans. Previously, he considered cutting away from the interview to stock footage of parades but decided they were cliché. He asked himself, "What types of pageants have we to relive wars?" and then recalled the annual Revolution reenactment. This scene is one of the documentary's most effective, questioning the value of man's military victories.

Erik Barnouw's short animated film, *Fable-Safe*, suggests this quest for victory has reached a point of no return. Unlike *Arms and Security*, *Fable-Safe* satirizes the "us" against "them" theme; the superpowers of the world panic and the film ends in holocaust.

Several times the material was so emotional and factual, however, that the speaker remained on camera throughout the interview; to have cutaways might have seriously detracted from the message. A good example occurs when Dr. Edward Teller appears. Dr. Teller, responding to questions concerning the overkill theory, looks directly into the camera and explains his thesis, without interruption. Benjamin permits Teller's statements to stand on their own; he refuses to employ angled shots or sudden transitions that might bias the scientist's presentation.

Occasionally, the film falters by assuming viewers possess ample information about various weapon systems; a more detailed analysis concerning the strategic value of each weapon might have clarified the issues relating to our defense program. The documentary does offer numerous visual aspects of the subject: missile launchings on land and under water, a 1955 Nevada atomic test in a created "town," a B-52 scramble practice alert, an ABM construction site and films of a metal mock-up of the B-1 bomber. The visualizations greatly assist producer Benjamin in his exploration of the complex issues surrounding the arms race and efforts to limit the production of nuclear weapons. By carefully reconstructing past events in a thorough, concise framework, the *Arms and Security* not only portrays the human condition at the time of its making but presents information that offers additional understanding of future nuclear endeavors.

24

JACK G. SHAHEEN

Only the Strong

Only the Strong is a highly professional, albeit opinionated, information film produced by the Institute for American Strategy (IAS) and sponsored by the American Security Council of Culpepper, Virginia. The institute's purpose is to strengthen national security, while the American Security Council has been campaigning since the early sixties to prevent arms limitations agreements with the Soviet Union.

Produced as a 16-mm color film which has a nominal rental fee, *Strong* is used extensively by church groups, veteran groups, service clubs, fraternal groups, and schools. The three commercial networks, however, refused to grant the IAS air time. (Normally it is network policy not to broadcast documentaries other than those produced and supervised by their own staff.) The IAS then approached local network affiliated stations and independents, which resulted in over four hundred stations telecasting *Strong* as a public service broadcast. The film was made available at no charge, whether broadcast on a sponsored or nonsponsored basis. *Strong* was shown over eight hundred times, more than half of those showings in prime time.[1]

Rival organizations such as the Center for Defense Information and the Arms Control Association petitioned to the television stations airing *Strong*, requesting reply time under provisions of the Federal Communications Commission's Fairness Doctrine. They contended *Strong* was more of a self-service and not a public service program.

Strong's narrator tells viewers they will be "taken inside the Soviet Union" for an in-depth view and that an objective analysis comparing the strategic capabilities of the United States and the Soviet Union will be presented. But in lieu of offering a factual or fair analysis, *Strong* proceeds to effectively propagandize its one-dimensional theme—the United States must maintain military superiority over Russia. It categorically claims that only power, especially nuclear power, is the path to peace.

Strong seeks to solicit public support for additional American arsenals. It offers clear-cut implications concerning the nature of a strong national security system with possession of ample atomic weapons. Implicit in the theme is the assumption that the bomb is the only entity preventing Soviet world conquest. The film fails to mention that the very presence of our nuclear weaponry might have directly led to a global buildup of nuclear arms (and, subsequently, a more fragile structure for maintaining world peace). *Strong*, however, considers Western weaponry a deterrent.

Secondly, by using primarily on-the-spot recording techniques, the film depicts the United States as the second most militarily powerful nation in the world. It effectively revives cold war paranoia, replacing reason and good judgment with fear and insecurity. In a deliberate, compelling style, *Strong* emphatically stresses that the Soviets are succeeding "in an all-out effort to overtake the United States." [2]

There are interviews with American military and congressional leaders, and stock footage from the Soviet Union. With the Russian footage, dramatic angle shots enhance the destructive power of Soviet warheads. The interviews, combined with shots of Russian weaponry, are carefully edited to convey *Strong*'s message: to ensure peace, the United States must strengthen its commitment to military superiority. One of those interviewed, George Champion, a member of the film's Blue Ribbon Defense Panel and former chairman of the Chase Manhattan Bank, states: "If the United States is not the strongest country in the world, world peace is in jeopardy."

Champion's statement accurately reflects the basic intent of the film: to promote patriotism through military might. *Strong*'s producers (there are no film credits; thus production personnel cannot be referred to by name) contend that the American dream of peace and prosperity can become a reality only if the United States immediately strengthens its arms supply. If not, they argue, total annihilation is imminent.

Strong shows people of different age groups being interviewed. It uses an on-the-street format, where individuals offer their views on whether the United States or the Soviet Union has military superiority. The film's narrator-interviewer is never seen. With the camera full on the interviewees, who seem unconcerned or uninformed, there is no consensus. The interview format is effective, giving the impression of a balanced approach to the complicated arms race issue. Just as the interviews conclude, the film's narrator states *Strong* will provide the true facts.

There are many visually impressive sequences in *Strong*, beginning with the opening graphic. White letters roll upward on a black background until the narrator states "only the strong survive." This dynamic introduction is followed immediately by abrasive jet sounds and visuals of bombers preparing for action.

The film's major asset is its visual impact. There are no subtle dissolves or slow fades, just quick cuts of exploding rockets and bombs. Following a montage of explosive action, there is a cut to a military general who warns, "If we don't take some action now, that's what's going to happen to us."

Camera angles are always upward, creating the effect of overwhelming Soviet power. To create a superior strength there are low-angle views of Russian warships anchored side by side in a seemingly endless line. The ships are viewed powering their way through heavy sea in clusters, to denote strength through sheer numbers. The colors are stark contrasts of red and black. Also featured are Russian submarines slicing their way through polar ice or ominously slithering through shrouds of fog. The sea action is accompanied by an eerie musical score, indicating a silent nemesis, lying in readiness for its unprepared victim.

A major portion of *Strong* is composed of stock footage of threatening Russian weaponry. The film clips from the Soviet Union were provided to the IAS by several film production agencies. Russian footage depicts an impregnable military force. There are shots of mobile missile launchers, hidden missile silos, strategic submarines, massive warships, advanced jet fighters, and marching troops at May Day celebrations. A montage of firing rockets and selected mock battle scenes add credibility to the narrator's statements about Soviet firepower; a ship, for example, is destroyed by an air-to-surface missile and a plane is easily struck down by air-to-air missiles.

In contrast to the action clips, a freeze frame of a Soviet SS-9 missile being paraded in Red Square is shown. The narrator stresses the megatonnage and makes a comparison with the Nagasaki bomb; the Russian weapon is 250 times greater. The sequences are skillfully edited to suggest that Russia possesses far more armaments than the United

States. Interestingly, the only footage of American weaponry is a bland orange shot of a model of a proposed B-1 bomber.

Strong neglects to present a broader interpretation of Soviet foreign policy during the early years of the cold war, proceeding on the narrow assumption that everything was "their" fault and not "ours." In this sense it becomes a propaganda film. Propaganda, having a rather broad meaning in this case, implies purposeful dissemination of information, hopefully to impress upon its viewers certain reactions which, from the viewpoint of the film maker, are desirable. On considering *Strong*'s intent, the IAS conclusion seems logical. The film, however, should be analyzed for what it is, instead of what it appears to be.

Because it is produced by the IAS, an arms lobby directed by former high-ranking military officers and key representatives of defense contractors, *Strong* lacks believability as an objective, factual presentation. The narrator's opening statement, which promises to show both Russian and American firepower, is empty rhetoric. Throughout the film, Russian military might is consistently depicted. Credibility is not further enhanced by the film's sponsors, the American Security Council, an anti-Communist group headed by several retired four-star generals and defense specialists.

Strong takes an extremely narrow view of the complex reasons behind the escalation of the nuclear arms buildup. Consequently, the film's conclusion is extremely limited and without scope—it suggests power is peace, lack of power is war (or worse yet, humiliating defeat and the threat of international Communism). Strong asks: "Do you want peace or war?" Viewers are given no alternatives. They are asked to accept the security of Hilaire Belloc's concept: Whatever happens, we have got The Maxim Gun and they have not.

Only the Strong has a limited perspective, presenting a one-dimensional point of view. Yet the film purports to be valid journalism by drawing on spokesmen from various disciplines of national leadership. Representatives from the military, the civilian sector, the executive branch of government, the scientific community, and the diplomatic corps are seen in quick succession to reinforce each other's viewpoints (for example, Foy D. Kohler, former ambassador to the Soviet Union; Dr. Edward Teller, "father of the H-bomb"; Gen. Lyman L. Lemnitzer, former chairman of the Joint Chiefs of Staff; Melvin Laird, former defense secretary; and Gen. Bruce Holloway). Each spokesman unanimously supports a massive American buildup. Each warns that an ongoing threat is posed by America's second rate power status against the Soviet Union. General Lemnitzer, for example, says, "The Soviets are not only matching us, they continue to forge ahead." This statement is explicitly detailed: the USSR has 350 submarines to our 100; they have 25 times as many radar installations, and 3000 fighter-interceptors to our 500 (by SALT we are limited to 1000 warheads, the Soviets have 2000). An avalanche of data numbs the viewer's perspective.

A *St. Louis Post-Dispatch* editorial contends the film's data is not totally accurate; *Strong* reveals that "the Russians have about five times as much missile megatonnage as we have, and thus could divide theirs into five times as many warheads as we have."[3] According to the newspaper's report, however, the United States "has a two-to-one lead in missile warheads and is expected to have a four-to-one lead by 1977."[4] In the ABC documentary *Arms and Security: How Much Is Enough?* (1972), narrator Frank Reynolds contends—

> It is estimated that the United States has enough nuclear power to destroy the major cities of the Soviet Union 34 times. She can destroy our major cities 13 times over. And it's getting more ominous. To all intents and purposes there are no secrets in science. For each time we escalate the arms race, each time we develop and build a more sophisticated weapons system, the Soviet Union matches us. And each time the Soviets start on a new weapons system, we follow suit. And so, the longer the arms race goes on, the less security we have, rather than more.[5]

Strong attempts to prove that America is the last defense against monolithic communism. Totally neglected is information concerned with the Free World's contribution to the arms stockpile. Completely ignored is any discussion of NATO's strategic strength (of which America is a substantial contributor) as well as the development of France and West Germany as nuclear powers. Also neglected is information pertaining to the ideological schism between the two giant Communist superpowers, the USSR and the People's Republic of China.

Strong was accepted as a "public service broadcast" by over four hundred American television stations, and telecast more than eight hundred times. Thomas A. Halstead, executive director of the Arms Control Association (ACA), spearheaded a drive for the opportunity to respond. Although the ACA and the Center for Defense Information did not offer rebuttals (they did not have a film of their own and, consequently, relied principally on individual appearances), they were largely responsible for two hundred television stations refusing to show the "biased, one-sided view of the international security situation which grossly exaggerates the military capabilities and intentions of the Soviet Union." [6]

At the film's conclusion, the narrator asks viewers to write in their opinions, affirmative or negative, to a "Peace Poll." The technique of soliciting viewer opinions via a Peace Poll is misleading. The Institute for American Strategy conveys the information contained in positive letters to members of Congress and the president. Those viewers who are undecided or those disagreeing with *Strong*'s message receive IAS materials designed to alter their beliefs.

Films such as *Only the Strong* are dangerous, not so much because of the information presented, but for the information not presented. When considering fairness and objectivity, the greatest deficiency of *Strong* is the absence of opposing commentary and footage of American military might. The film deliberately avoids mentioning our defensive and offensive capabilities. There is no discussion of the motivation and the cause-and-effect cycle essential to any understanding of the arms race. [7] Instead, *Strong* creates fear in the psyche of viewers. It is effective propaganda produced not to offer a balanced perspective of complex issues but to support the self-serving interest of the military spending lobby.

25 DONALD BITTNER

And When the War Is Over—The American Military in the 70's

Commercial television in the United States may be defined as an entertainment medium owned by corporations whose primary goal is to make profits through entertainment aimed at mass audiences. Thus, the American viewing public is subjected to large amounts of programming, generally of a low cultural and intellectual level. Occasionally, the networks do provide "higher levels" of programming. The series "NBC Reports" is one such offering that attempts to present quality programming to small, selective audiences. In January and February of 1973, "NBC Reports" presented a two-part NBC White Paper produced by Fred Freed, entitled, *And When the War Is Over—The American Military in the 70's*. The aim of this essay is to examine part one of the documentary, which deals with our country's nuclear forces, and to determine if this complex topic could be treated successfully in prime time.

One major problem with *War Is Over* is its failure to state and follow a specific purpose. The documentary contains a series of loosely structured episodes illustrating a number of interviews, meaningless statistics, overt, unsubstantiated biases, and large quantities of footage showing bombers at various stages of flight. Early in the program, the narrator, Floyd Kalber, said: "The odds that our nuclear weapons will never be used grows, and we will only have to use them once to destroy ourselves. What do we want to do about them? What do we want from them?" But Kalber's thoughtful questions are never answered. The program does little to enlighten, educate, or inform an audience about the American and Soviet nuclear deterrent. Instead, it develops into a personal essay full of assumptions and prejudices.

The documentary is a classic example of a complex problem presented in an oversimplified manner. Telecasts of this nature tend only to reinforce opinions already in the minds of viewers. To adequately produce a program about nuclear warfare and the nuclear arms race, a considerable amount of research and effort is required. Each complicated nuclear aspect would have to be examined in detail. But television network systems could never complete such a thorough project successfully; the viewing audience would be too small and commercial profits so minimal that the networks could not justify the time and expense. To support the contention that excessive commercialism negates the presentation of purportedly thoughtful documentaries, *War Is Over* will be examined from several viewpoints relating to: the role of change in the modern world, the historical perspective, and the issue of broadcast journalism.

Since the industrial revolution, the world has been subject to rapid change—in transportation, communication, industrial production, and warfare. Science and technology have presented the human race with many material advantages but also newer and more effective means of destruction. Although we accept many aspects of our changing world, there has been a reluctance to accept this concept of change as it relates to warfare.

War Is Over offered evidence of two tendencies: to seemingly accept the changes in warfare since the advent of the nuclear age, but to make a presentation often predicated upon rejection of the changes. For example, the program notes there are three paradoxes of the nuclear stalemate: 1) that we have become used to it; 2) to deter an attack, our potential opponent must know that no matter how successful his attack may be, the United States will be able to retaliate with enough force to ensure the attacker's destruction; 3) each year we develop more weapons, and each year we are less secure. The documentary then reverts back to change since World War II, noting that in 1940 the United States had the eighteenth largest army in the world. Subsequently, a list of meaningless statistics on the growth of the Department of Defense and the Pentagon is given. Nothing is said of the real changes and the subsequent need of military preparedness then and now. Emphasis is given to the past. For example, in any major conflict up to 1940, the United States could slowly retool for war behind our navy and the vast expanses of the Atlantic and Pacific oceans. This is what occurred in World War II; it took the United States four years to retool and mobilize to the point where we could meet the major enemies in decisive combat, defeat their armies, and occupy their countries. But nuclear preparedness is another matter.

Despite the dislike for a balance of terror, many believe our nuclear strategic reserve is inadequate. There is nothing "divinely preordained" that the United States, the West, or the Western civilization will win any conflict because our side is always "just." Potential enemies are also working on means of defense and are further developing their offensive weapons. They influence what will occur, but this stimulus to all of our activity was never examined in the program. Our activity depends on Soviet and Chinese military and foreign policies, what weapons they have and will possess in the future.

Are we as secure as we believe? As time goes on, do we become accustomed to nuclear threats? Do our chances of surviving a nuclear attack lessen with time? In this documentary, Congressman Les Aspin said, "There is a threat, but we have more than enough to meet that threat. We have enough to meet any threat." This is a basic assumption, but a dangerous one on which to base any policy. The question is "for how long?" Technology, research, and development can quickly change and negate any weapons lead. What is the time from initial conception of a weapons system to research and development to mass production to the troops receiving it? Congressman Aspin also noted that "the real question about the Defense Department budget is the simple question of how much is enough. . . . and it really is a question of judgment." How much money should be spent on the military and research and development of new weapons? Part of the change since 1945 is that it is strictly a question of judgment, and if a wrong decision is made, there is no second opportunity to recover.

The key is change—change in the basic underlying rules of great power politics and in technology. The game of international politics is played by rules that all members know and to which they adhere. One new rule is that the basic function of strategic nuclear weapons is fulfilled if they are not used. Mr. Kalber noted that, "We go on spending money for weapons we can never expect to use." This "change" in military procedure is what keeps this country "safe." Nuclear weapons may cost more money, be more complex, and harder to understand, but these weapons will have failed in their ultimate purpose if potential nuclear opponents launch a nuclear attack on the United States. Their primary function is to prevent such an attack.

Another aspect of change, an outgrowth of World War II, is the utter impersonality of killing and destruction. The impersonality of B-52 conventional bombing of North Vietnam or artillerymen firing howitzers at an unseen enemy several miles away pales into insignificance when compared to impersonalization in nuclear warfare. This aspect is only casually mentioned in *War Is Over*. There is no elaboration of significance of the increased change; Mr. Kalber only notes that we can kill one hundred million Russians with an unspoken acknowledgment —they can retaliate.

This whole aspect was unintentionally but briefly touched on in act 4 when the program shifted to an interview with Lt. Michael Durfor, an air force officer stationed at a missile silo in Minot, North Dakota. Kalber asked Durfor: "How is part of this rain of death to be launched and inflicted on the enemy?" Lieutenant Durfor replied: "The process is quite simple. The men would have to take keys from separate safes. They would have to go to a position twelve feet apart. They would have to return their keys no more than two seconds apart." The result would launch ten missiles controlled by the capsule, ten ICBMs with a total of thirty warheads, with each warhead ten times as powerful as the Hiroshima bomb. Constant reference is made to the power of the Hiroshima atomic bombs without explanation. To assume that the entire viewing audience knows the power of the Hiroshima bomb and its significance is truly frightening. The new philosophy of war, due to advances in technology, is not really analyzed further.

Nuclear weapons have made us safe for thirty years. But other types of warfare have been used—the limited war of Korea and the conflict in Vietnam involving the great powers are costly and always represent the danger of escalating into major conflicts. These types of wars and even terrorist activities occur beneath the nuclear umbrella.

The conflict continues. This is true of any struggle involving client states of great powers who do not possess great numbers of nuclear weapons. The nuclear country of Israel and the nonnuclear Arab states threaten to embroil the United States and the Soviet Union in a major conflict; India and Pakistan pose the threat of a major conflict escalating between the Soviet Union and China.

Despite the major emphasis on change, there are several subtle conditions not new to this decade or generation. Obviously these are not the two traditional military evaluations of weapons but rather several other points that were not discussed in the documentary. On the contrary, implications in the program were that somehow several problems, which are not new, in fact, have developed in the nuclear age.

The narrator emphasized money being spent on weapons and that the numerical increase of weapons did not produce a "safe" feeling in the country. In act 1, Kalber noted, "each year we have more weapons; each year we are less safe." In the next act, he repeats, "So, we spend billions of dollars, the Russians spend billions of rubles, and in the end we are less secure than when we started." But does this information reveal anything new? Can current generations feel unique in feeling insecurity despite heavy investments? The answer is obviously no. Two important examples in this century illustrated this dilemma. In 1906, the British Royal Navy launched a new class of battleship, H.M.S. *Dreadnaught*, with greater tonnage, thicker armor, larger guns, and faster speed than any other battleship then in commission; all other capital ships immediately became obsolete. The British proceeded to build more ships and improved on the initial design. Did their feelings of "security" grow as the Royal Navy grew in strength? Britain's potential enemy, Imperial Germany, also began constructing better ships. Actually, greater feelings of insecurity were experienced when the British launched the *Dreadnaught*. Even when World War I commenced, these ships failed to offer a sense of security. They had cost so much and taken so long to build that, especially in Britain, the belief was that the national existence rested on their very existence. Eventually they became too valuable to risk in an all-out major naval engagement.

In the interwar period, for example, France was obsessed by security from the German menace to the east of her borders. Invaded twice within seventy years, defeated once in 1870 and almost defeated in World War I, suffering tremendous casualties and material losses in these two wars, the fear of another German invasion, and the added anxiety of the possibility of fighting the dreaded Germans alone obsessed France. In 1929, a major shift in French military policy occurred with the decision to build the Maginot Line. France retreated into a "Fortress France," investing millions in the expensive construction of a line of fortifications running the entire length of the French-German border. But, the French still did not feel secure against the German threat, which was to loom after 1933.

An argument can be made that the anxieties facing the British and French were not the same as those that exist today. This may be true, but the people of that time probably viewed their threats as we perceive the nuclear threat today. Feelings of insecurity, despite millions invested in various weapons, are nothing new.

Another factor of continuity concerns an interpretation of the SALT agreements signed in 1972. Kalber noted that with the agreements, certain implications would result for the United States and the Soviet Union. "This would make their cities and the people in them nuclear hostages," said Kalber. This point was further elaborated in a filmed seminar at North Carolina State University. There Mr. Albert Carnesola, a staff member of the SALT negotiating team, said in response to a student comment: "I don't think it's obvious to the average American citizen that he is now . . . and that he (will always) be a hostage to the offensive weapons of the Soviet Union and that will deter war."

Carnesola's analysis is substantially correct. But this has been the situation since the Soviet Union joined the nuclear club in 1949. The whole basis of "balance of terror" rests on the foundation of each side being able to retaliate against the other in case of attack. It is the traditional concept of massive retaliation, which in essence has always held the industrial and population centers of a potential enemy as hostage in return for the more restrained policies of their governments.

Air power enthusiasts of the post–World War I era and the World War II period had similar thoughts. With the development of large strategic bombers, a theory was developed that either could make war too costly for the combatants or, once engaged in, would quickly be ended by strategic bombing attacks. The idea was simple: with a fleet of large, manned strategic bombers capable of attacking urban and industrial areas of any country, any nation would be open to quick attack and annihilation if the bombers got through. At best, if all sides held such weapons, the cities and industrial areas of the states would be hostages to each other. At worst, the side with inferior arms, believing the potential enemy had bombing superiority, would be dangerously threatened.

In the 1930s Stanley Baldwin, the British prime minister, said in the House of Commons, "The bombers will always get through." This statement had tremendous implications. Britain was later confronted with a problem of believing that this was the case when Nazi aggression occurred. The country did not possess the required defenses against bombers, either to locate and attack the potential incoming German planes or the capability of attacking German industrial and urban areas in retaliation (The development of the Fighter Command organization was then only occurring and being refined during the Munich period, and the capability of Bomber Command at this time was likewise limited).

In addition to other factors concerning the Munich policy of the British Government, the lack of an adequate strategic bombing force influenced British policy. The key point, however, is that the hostage system was implicit in the theories developed by air power enthusiasts after World War I. The larger bombers, missiles, and nuclear weapons are only the most recent developments that fulfilled air power theories to their furthest extension.

The concept of our cities being hostaged to Soviet power is established fact. What has changed is that technology and research have been on the threshold of being able to develop a series of defensive weapons against nuclear offensive weapons. The cost in money, material, and time, however, would have been prohibitive. The SALT agreements are a basic understanding not to waste funds and material on the construction of these systems which, at the same time, would have involved further expenditure of funds for research and development of new offensive weapons to counter the newly developed defensive ones. An agreement had been reached to retain in essence the "hostage system," which had been in effect in one form or another between the Soviet Union and the United States since 1949. In this sense, the speed and development, as a result of change, was negated by an informal agreement to maintain the status quo—each nation's population and industrial centers would remain hostages as they have for the past twenty-four years, but now officially sanctioned by the two great powers.

In addition to certain defects in the presentation and analysis of the problems of nuclear weapons (that have no real relation to the all-encompassing title of the program), there is another point of view that should be considered in *War Is Over*. Ineptness in production ranged from script to interviews and the filming. The constant repetition of B-52s taking off, with cuts to children at play while the narrator discusses the perils of nuclear warfare, was annoying and contributed nothing to understanding the problems of nuclear warfare. Other questionable aspects included the filming of a seminar at North Carolina State University, whose contribution to the issue being discussed is questionable interviewing. The technique of asking leading questions to solicit expected responses occurred. For example, in act 1 at Strategic

Command headquarters, Alvin Davis interviewed Gen. J. C. Meyer, commander in chief of the Strategic Air Command. The question posed by Mr. Davis was: "Is there any doubt in your mind, sir, that the bombers would drop their bombs despite the fact that they would know their own country was probably already in ruins?" General Meyer replied: "I do not have the slightest shadow of a doubt that every missile crew and bomber crew would perform the mission that it has been trained to do, when so directed by the President of the United States." What other reply could General Meyer give? To answer in any other way would expose himself to grave doubts about his own leadership and the reliability of the United States' strategic deterrent.

Another instance occurred in act 4 during the interview with Lieutenant Durfor. Alvin Davis was again the interviewer. The subject: the possible launching of the ICBMs in case of a Soviet attack on the United States. The following questions and responses were heard—

> DAVIS: "Would you fire if the order came?"
> DURFOR: "Yes."
> DAVIS: "Would you hesitate?"
> DURFOR: "No."
> DAVIS: "Would you turn the key?"
> DURFOR: "Yes."

The lieutenant has been trained and assigned a mission, he could give no answers other than those he gave.

Similar questions exposed other flaws in the documentary. It was stated that Lieutenant Durfor had never fired an ICBM in combat, nor in practice. He had not, in essence, been at war. On its higher strategic level, questions of the type posed to Lieutenant Durfor are similar to asking an infantryman who has never experienced combat what he expects to do when he first engages the enemy. It is an unfair question. No one knows how he will react in any combat situation, strategic or tactical. Before combat, assumptions are made that men trained to perform certain tasks or missions will do so. But no one knows until the event arrives what exactly will occur.

Several instances of unbalanced presentation were in evidence. One focused on a discussion with Maj. Gen. Timothy Dacey, USAF (Retired), about the operation and concept of the Strategic Airborne Command's headquarters, code-named *Looking Glass* (General Dacey flew for a number of years in *Looking Glass* as commander of the flight).

The narrator noted that "every time he had to believe that before it was over he might have to give the order that would destroy half the world." Nothing was mentioned as to why General Dacey would have had to give such a command—the Soviets would have attacked first.

Considerable emphasis was devoted to Congressman Aspin's ideas that the secretary of defense and the chairman of the Joint Chiefs of Staff control congressional proceedings. Aspin said these men had the distinct "psychological advantage" as all the figures and resources of the Department of Defense were at their disposal and yet committee members had only five minutes to question them. Some analysis here would have been appropriate, since its implications for the doctrine of civilian control of the military and the power of Congress over military affairs and related financial matters are considerable.

Contrasting views should have been presented. A Marine Corps general explained to the author the exact opposite position. Noting that members of various committees before which the Department of Defense and military personnel had to appear and testify were named by knowledgeable professional members of Congress, witnesses appearing before them had to know their material and have conceptualized it before they appeared. Committee members, instead of being at a "psychological disadvantage," were in control of the proceedings. They knew their business, they were experts in military affairs, and could offer strong criticism to anyone not properly prepared. Whether the general's view could be accepted by the program's producers is not important. What is significant is that no contrasting view was shown to counter Congressman Aspin's ideas. Instead, the viewing audience witnessed brief excerpts of former Secretary of Defense Melvin Laird and chairman of the Joint Chiefs of Staff, Admiral Thomas Moorer, defending requests for additional funds. They referred to Soviet challenges, accomplishments, capabilities, the implication being that justification for support was manufactured at budget time to buttress requests for additional funds.

Finally, the parade of various statistics developed into meaningless data, which eventually boggled the mind. Kalber presented a continuous flow of data ranging from the number of nuclear-carrying aircraft and submarines the United States possesses to the number of cups of coffee consumed each day in the Pentagon. The information presented only vague impressions.

Subjects such as nuclear warfare are not suitable for presentation on

commercial television unless there is thorough preparation and an allot-
ment of considerable telecasting time. There was one positive aspect
to *War Is Over*—it presented some of the men involved in the manning
of the nation's strategic nuclear reserve as human beings attempting
to do a job. As General Dacey said, "I'm not a Jack D. Ripper or
Dr. Strangelove. I, like my fellows in SAC, we're just a bunch of
guys trying to do a job, and ready to do a job, and hoping we'd never
have to do it."

The major reason the documentary failed is because it lacked a unified theme. No purpose, aim, or goal was stated. The title promised
an examination of the American military in the 1970s. In the introduction, it appeared an orientation concerning nuclear warfare would be
given. Instead, the program wandered aimlessly, offering perspectives
on past military accomplishments, interviews with diverse individuals
interspaced with Sunday newsclippings, scenes of the bombers taking
off and landing, and views of life on military bases.

In conclusion, considerable thought and perspective is necessary
when producing documentaries related to nuclear war. Modern warfare
is a highly complicated subject, involving interlocking relationships
between the military, government, technology, industry, and society.
Any attempt to present nuclear war in a simplified form with simplistic
answers ultimately does a great disservice. If nuclear warfare is to be
properly explored, a commitment to a series of programs investigating
all aspects of nuclear war and defense, disarmament, the strategic
deterrent, the men who make policies and man the forces, the interlocking relationships, and the basic agreements for and against nuclear
deterrent would have to be presented. Such an effort would require
considerable funding, a great and balanced effort and dedication of all
concerned. Yet if the documentaries were produced, it is doubtful large
audiences would view them. Here is another paradox (that Kalber did
not mention). If the world has come to learn to live with the balance
of terror and all that it implies, it may also have come to be bored by
it all.

Distributors and Credits

The distribution company for each film is listed here, with approval of agency representatives.

Above and Beyond
   Films Incorporated
   733 Greenbay Road
   Wilmette, Illinois 60019

And When the War Is Over—The American Military in the 70's
   NBC-TV
   30 Rockefeller Plaza
   New York, New York 10020

Arms and Security: How Much Is Enough? (for sale only)
   ABC News, Television Documentary Programs
   7 West Sixty-sixth Street
   New York, New York 10023

The Atom Strikes
   Tobyhanna Army Depot
   DR Film Distribution/Utilization Branch
   Warehouse 3, Bay 3
   Tobyhanna, Pennsylvania 18466

The Bedford Incident
   MacMillan Audio Brandon
   34 MacQueston Parkway South
   Mt. Vernon, New York 10550

The Beginning or the End
    Screen Gems, Inc.
    729 Seventh Avenue
    New York, New York 10019

Building the Bomb
    Time-Life Films, Inc.
    Time-Life Building
    Rockefeller Center
    New York, New York 10020

Countdown to Zero (NBC 1966)
    NBC-TV
    30 Rockefeller Plaza
    New York, New York 10020

The Day the Earth Caught Fire
    Twyman Films, Inc.
    329 Salem Avenue
    Dayton, Ohio 45401

The Decision to Drop the Bomb
    Films Incorporated
    733 Greenbay Road
    Wilmette, Illinois 60019

Dr. Strangelove
    Columbia Cinematheque
    711 Fifth Avenue
    New York, New York 10022
    or
    Swank Motion Pictures, Inc.
    201 South Jefferson Avenue
    St. Louis, Missouri 63166

Fail Safe
    Contemporary/McGraw Hill
    1221 Avenue of the Americas
    New York, New York 10020
    or
    Twyman Films, Inc.
    329 Salem Avenue
    Dayton, Ohio 45401

Five
>Silvermine Films
>49 West Forty-fifth Street
>New York, New York 10018
>*or*
>Columbia Pictures International Corporation
>Subsidiary of Columbia Pictures
>711 Fifth Avenue
>New York, New York 10022

Footnotes on the Atomic Age
>NBC-TV
>30 Rockefeller Plaza
>New York, New York 10020

H-Bomb over U.S.
>MacMillan Audio Brandon
>34 MacQuestion Parkway South
>Mt. Vernon, New York 10550

Hiroshima: A Document of the Atomic Bombing
>The Educational Center
>University of Michigan
>416 Fourth Street
>Ann Arbor, Michigan 48104

Hiroshima, Mon Amour
>Contemporary/McGraw Hill
>1221 Avenue of the Americas
>New York, New York 10020

Hiroshima-Nagasaki ("NET Journal" 283)
>NET Television Incorporated
>2715 Packard Road
>Ann Arbor, Michigan 48104

Hiroshima-Nagasaki—August, 1945
>Center for Mass Communications of Columbia University
>136 South Broadway
>Irvington-on-Hudson
>New York, New York 10533

The Hole
>John Hubley
>165 East Seventy-second
>New York, New York 10021

or
MacMillan Audio Brandon
34 MacQueston Parkway South
Mt. Vernon, New York 10550

Ladybug, Ladybug
United Artists, 16
729 Seventh Avenue
New York, New York 10019

Only the Strong
Institute for American Strategy
Boston, Virginia 22713

On the Beach
United Artists
729 Seventh Avenue
New York, New York 10019

Panic in Year Zero
United Films
1425 South Main
Tulsa, Oklahoma 74119

Rumours of War (for sale only)
Time-Life Films, Inc.
Time-Life Building
Rockefeller Center
New York, New York 10020

A Short Vision
Films Incorporated
733 Greenbay Road
Wilmette, Illinois 60019
or
EBE
425 North Michigan Avenue
Chicago, Illinois 60611

A Tale of Two Cities
U.S. Atomic Energy Commission
Technical Film Library
P.O. Box 63
Oak Ridge, Tennessee 37830

A Thousand Cranes: Children of Hiroshima
    MacMillan Audio Brandon
    34 MacQueston Parkway South
    Mt. Vernon, New York 10550

To Die, To Live (for sale only)
    Time-Life Films, Inc.
    Time-Life Building
    Rockefeller Center
    New York, New York 10020

23 Skidoo
    Contemporary/McGraw Hill
    1221 Avenue of the Americas
    New York, New York 10020

The War Game
    Contemporary/McGraw Hill
    1221 Avenue of the Americas
    New York, New York 10020

The World, the Flesh, and the Devil
    Films Incorporated
    733 Greenbay Road
    Wilmette, Illinois 60019

Credits: Feature Films

Above and Beyond (1953)
Produced and directed by Melvin Frank and Norman Panama
Screenplay by Melvin Frank, Norman Panama, and Beirne Lay, Jr.
A Metro-Goldwyn-Mayer Picture
Cast: Robert Taylor
       Eleanor Parker
       James Whitmore
       Larry Keating

The Bedford Incident (1965)
Produced and directed by James B. Harris
Screenplay by James Poe
Original book by Mark Rascovich
A Columbia Picture
Cast: Richard Widmark
       Sidney Poitier

James MacArthur
Martin Balsam
Wally Cox
Eric Portman

The Beginning or the End (1946)
Produced by Samuel Marx
Directed by Norman Taurog
Screenplay by Frank Wead
Original story by Robert Considine
A Metro-Goldwyn-Mayer Picture
Cast: Brian Donlevy
        Robert Walker
        Tom Drake
        Beverly Tyler
        Audrey Totter
        Hume Cronyn

The Day the Earth Caught Fire (1962)
Produced and directed by Val Guest
Screenplay by Wolf Mankowitz and Val Guest
A Universal-International Picture
Cast: Edward Judd
        Janet Munro
        Leo McKern
        Arthur Christiansen
        Reginald Beckwith

Dr. Strangelove (1964)
Produced and directed by Stanley Kubrick
Screenplay by Stanley Kubrick, Terry Southern, and Peter George
Original book by Peter George
A Columbia Picture
Cast: Peter Sellers
        George C. Scott
        Sterling Hayden
        Keenan Wynn
        Slim Pickens

Fail Safe (1964)
Produced by Max Youngstein
Directed by Sidney Lumet
Screenplay by Walter Bernstein

Original book by Eugene Burdick and Harvey Wheeler
A Columbia Picture
Cast: Henry Fonda
Dan O'Herlihy
Walter Matthau
Frank Overton
Fritz Weaver
Edward Binns

Five (1951)
Produced, written, and directed by Arch Oboler
A Columbia Picture
Cast: William Phipps
Susan Douglas
James Anderson
Charles Lampkin
Earl Lee

Hiroshima, Mon Amour (1959)
Produced and directed by Alain Resnais
Screenplay by Marguerite Duras
A Zenith International Picture
Cast: Emmanuelle Riva
Eiji Okada
Stella Dassas
Pierre Barbaud
Bernard Fresson

Ladybug, Ladybug (1963)
Produced and directed by Frank Perry
Screenplay by Eleanor Perry
Original article by Lois Dickert
A United Artists Picture
Cast: Jane Connell
William Daniels
James Frawley
Richard Hamilton
Kathryn Hays

On the Beach (1959)
Produced and directed by Stanley Kramer
Screenplay by John Paxton
Original story by Nevil Shute

A United Artists Picture
Cast: Gregory Peck
        Ava Gardner
        Fred Astaire
        Anthony Perkins
        Donna Anderson

Panic in Year Zero (1962)
Produced by Lou Rusoff and Arnold Houghland
Directed by Ray Milland
Screenplay by Jay Simms and John Morton
An American International Picture
Cast: Ray Milland
        Jean Hagen
        Frankie Avalon
        Mary Mitchell
        Richard Bakalyan

The World, the Flesh, and the Devil (1959)
Produced by George Englund
Directed by Ranald MacDougall
Screenplay by Ferdinand Reyher
Original story by Mathew Phipps Shiel
A Metro-Goldwyn-Mayer Picture
Cast: Harry Belafonte
        Inger Stevens
        Mel Ferrer

Credits: Documentaries and Educational Short Films

And When the War Is Over: The American Military in the 70's (1973)
Produced by Fred Freed
Reported and narrated by Floyd Kalber

Arms and Security: How Much Is Enough? (1972)
Produced and written by James Benjamin
Reported and narrated by Frank Reynolds
Directed by Howard Enders
ABC-TV

The Atom Strikes (1946) and *A Tale of Two Cities* (1946)
Produced by the United States Army Films
Distributed by the National Auto Visual Center, Washington, D.C.

Countdown to Zero (1966)
Produced and written by Fred Freed
Reported by Chet Huntley and Elie Abel

The Decision to Drop the Bomb (1965)
NBC-TV
Produced by Fred Freed   Associate, Len Giovannitti
Executive Producer, Irving Gitlin

Footnotes on the Atomic Age (1969)
Directed by Walter C. Miller
Narrated and written by Tom Pettit
NBC-TV

H-Bomb over U.S. (1962)
Produced by the Center for the Study of Democratic Institutions
Directed by George Zabriskie

Hiroshima: A Document of the Atomic Bombing (1970)
Produced for Japanese television by Nippon Eiga Shinsha, Ltd.,
Tokyo, Japan

Hiroshima-Nagasaki ("NET Journal" [1970])
Produced by William Weston
Narrated by Richard McCutchen
National Educational Television
Note: Two of the three segments in the NET documentary were obtained from
        outside sources. Segment one, *Hiroshima-Nagasaki—August, 1945*
        was produced by Professor Erik Barnouw, written, edited, and conar-
        rated by Paul Ronder; Center for Mass Communications of Columbia
        University Press. Segment two, *Building the Bomb* was produced by
        R. W. Reed and written by Anthony Jay for BBC-TV.

Hiroshima-Nagasaki—August, 1945 (1970)
Produced by Professor Erik Barnouw
Narrated by Paul Ronder and Kazuko Oshima
Written and edited by Paul Ronder

The Hole (1962)
Produced and directed by John and Faith Hubley
Improvised dialogue by Dizzy Gillespie and George Mathews

Only the Strong (1972)
Produced and distributed by the Institute for American Strategy
Boston, Virginia

Rumours of War (1972)
Produced by BBC-TV and distributed by Time-Life Films, Inc.
Produced and Directed by Peter Jones
Narrated by Paul Vaughan

A Short Vision (1956)
Produced, written, and directed by Joan and Peter Foldes
Narrated by James McKehnie

A Thousand Cranes: Children of Hiroshima (1962)
Written and directed by Betty Jean Lifton
Photography by Akinori Fujii

To Die, To Live (1975)
Written and directed by Robert Vas
BBC-TV

23 Skidoo (1964)
Produced and directed by Julian Biggs
The National Film Board of Canada
Edited by Julian Biggs and Kathleen Shannon

The War Game (1966)
Directed and produced by Peter Watkins
BBC-TV

Notes

Preface

1. Dorothy B. Jones, "The Hollywood War Film: 1942–1944," *Hollywood Quarterly*, October 1945, p. 1.
2. Alfred Bester, "Air Power; Epic and Adventure," *Holiday*, January 1957, p. 99.
3. Statement made by Dale Wile, National Educational Television: reply to correspondence (Ann Arbor, Mich., 19 December 1972).
4. David A. Sohn, *Film: The Creative Eye* (Dayton: George A. Pflaum, 1970). p. x.
5. Robert Heyer and Anthony Meyer, *Discovery in Film* (New York: Paulist Press, 1967), p. 19.

1. The Beginning or the End

1. "The Beginning or the End," *Time*, 24 February 1947, p. 106.
2. "The Beginning or the End," *Life*, 17 March 1947, p. 75.
3. David Manning White and Richard Averson, *The Celluloid Weapon* (Boston: Beacon Press, 1972), p. 130.
4. *Life*, pp. 75–78.
5. Ted Sennet, ed., *The Movie Buff's Book* (New York: Pyramid Books, 1975), p. 25.
6. *Time*, p. 106.
7. *Life*, p. 76.
8. Ibid.
9. David Wallechinsky and Irving Wallace, *The People's Almanac* (New York: Doubleday, Inc., 1975), p. 242.
10. William G. Ward, *My Kingdom for Just One Strackeljahn* (New York: Richard Rosen Press, 1972), p. 111.
11. James M. Martin, "The Best of All Impossible Worlds," *American Film Journal of the Film and Television Arts*, March 1976, pp. 30, 31.
12. Charles Barry, ed., *Collier's Yearbook, 1947* (New York: Collier and Son Corp., 1947), p. 49.

13. *Time*, p. 106.

14. Ibid.

15. *Life*, p. 75.

16. Gene Shrader, "Atomic Doubletalk," *Center Magazine*, January–February 1971, p. 31.

17. Gordon C. Zahn, ed., *Thomas Merton on Peace* (New York: McCalls, 1969), p. 7.

18. *Life*, p. 78.

19. "Hollywood's Atomic Dud," *Newsweek*, 3 March 1947, p. 81.

20. *Time*, p. 106.

2. Five

1. Andrew Sarris, *The American Cinema* (New York: E. P. Dutton, Inc., 1968), p. 264.

2. John Baxter, *Science Fiction in the Cinema* (New York: A. S. Barnes, 1970), p. 156.

3. Robert Hughes, ed., *Film: Book II—Films of Peace and War* (New York: Grove Press, Inc., 1962), p. 10.

4. "Glen and Randa," *Film Facts* (1971):577, 578.

5. Robert Hatch, "The Garden of Atom," *New Republic*, 14 May 1951, p. 23.

6. Hughes, p. 107.

3. Hiroshima, Mon Amour

1. Lee R. Bobker, *Elements of Film* (Chicago: Harcourt Brace & World, Inc., 1969), p. 30.

2. Ibid., p. 223.

3. John Simon, *Private Screenings* (New York: Berkeley Medallion, 1967), p. 244.

4. Bobker, p. 155.

4. The World, the Flesh, and the Devil

1. The author perused critical writings from *Film Facts* 2: 20, 17 June 1959, pp. 105–6; *Variety*, 8 April 1959; *Time*, 1 June 1959; *New York Times*, 21 May 1959; *New York Herald Tribune*, 21 May 1959; and *Saturday Review*, 2 May 1959.

2. "The World, the Flesh, and the Devil," *London Times*, 7 September 1959, p. 3C.

3. Paul V. Beckley, "The World, the Flesh, and the Devil." *New York Herald Tribune*, 21 May 1959, p. 23.

4. "The World, the Flesh, and the Devil," *Monthly Film Bulletin*, September 1959, p. 121.

5. Bosley Crowther, "The World, the Flesh, and the Devil," *New York Times*, 21 May 1959, p. 35.

6. Albert Johnson, "Beige, Brown, or Black," *Film Quarterly*, Fall 1959, p. 43.

7. Hollis Alpert, "All This and Heaven Too," *Saturday Review*, 2 May 1959, p. 31.

5. *On the Beach*

1. Pauline Kael, *Kiss, Kiss, Bang, Bang* (Boston: Little, Brown and Co., 1965), p. 207.
2. John Howard Lawson, *Film: The Creative Process* (New York: Hill and Wang, 1964), p. 160.
3. Arthur Knight, "Not With a Bang or a Whimper," *Saturday Review*, 24 October 1959, pp. 32, 33.
4. Ibid.
5. "On the Beach," *Time*, 29 December 1959, p. 44.
6. Robert Hughes, ed., *Film: Book II—Films of Peace and War* (New York: Grove Press, 1962), p. 171.
7. Cleveland Amory, "A Director Who Conveys a Message," *St. Louis Globe Democrat*, 21 October 1976, p. 22A.
8. Nevil Shute, *On the Beach* (New York: Signet Books, 1958), p. 229.
9. Bosley Crowther, "On the Beach," *New York Times*, 18 December 1959, p. 34.
10. Lawson, p. 161.

8. *Ladybug, Ladybug*

1. "Invasion U.S.A.", *New York Times*, 30 April 1953, p. 39.
2. Caryl Rivers, "Hip Deep in the Real Fifties," *World*, 8 May 1973, pp. 29, 30.
3. John Simon, *Private Screenings* (New York: Berkeley Medallion Books, 1967), p. 121.
4. Ibid.
5. Rivers, p. 30.
6. Bosley Crowther, "*Ladybug, Ladybug*," *New York Times*, 24 December 1963, p. 9.
7. Ibid.
8. Ibid.

9. *Dr. Strangelove Or: How I Learned to Stop Worrying and Love the Bomb*

1. General Walker ran for governor of Texas. Though the Belden Poll showed he would come in last in a field of five, he claimed that he would win, since the public, even as they *claimed* they would vote for other candidates, gave him "the secret wink." General Walker later became nationally known when it was alleged that Lee Harvey Oswald had attempted to assassinate him.
2. I say two of the films, since the constant overstressing of "Waltzing Matilda" detracts from *On the Beach*. I have remarked elsewhere that Stanley Kramer seems to be making a career of foreground music and background visuals. See George W. Linden, "Ten Questions about Film Form," *Journal of Aesthetic Education* 5, no. 2, (April 1971):61–73.
3. The extension of theme beyond plot is even more apparent in *2001: A Space Odyssey*. If one pays much attention to the plot in *2001*, he misses 90 percent of the film. The thematic essence of *2001* is a fervent affirmation of hope in the future of man.

4. These repeated intercuts were later used by Antonioni in one of his least successful films: *Zabriski Point*. Antonioni recurrently blows up a house at the end of the film.

5. The dancing or "waltzing" quality is later used by Kubrick in *2001* when he conjoins the "The Blue Danube" (audio) with the movements of the spaceships (visual).

6. This concern with the future is the substance of both *2001* and *A Clockwork Orange*. The great chandelier in the War Room in *Strangelove* may be a Kubrick Mandala. He repeats this form in the space station of *2001*.

7. Robert Hatch, review in *Nation*, 3 February 1964, pp. 127, 128.

8. In 1973 there were seven thousand murders in the United States; thirty-seven in Japan.

10. Fail Safe

1. "The Day the Bomb Fell," *Time*, 9 October 1964, p. 109.

2. Ibid.

3. Roy Huss and Norman Silverstein, *The Film Experience* (New York: Dell Publishing, 1968), p. 52.

4. Eugene Burdick and Harvey Wheeler, *Fail Safe* (New York: McGraw Hill, 1962), pp. 277, 278.

5. Albert Einstein's book contains much of his philosophy regarding the use of atomic energy. Gen. Douglas MacArthur's book, *A Soldier Speaks: Public Papers and Speeches of General of the Army Douglas MacArthur*, contains speeches in which he voiced his concern regarding the nuclear arms race.

6. *Present at the Creation*, the 1970 Pulitzer prize-winning book by former Secretary of State Dean Acheson, provides an inside look at events that led to the decision to enter a full-scale nuclear arms race with the development of the hydrogen bomb.

12. A Thousand Cranes: Children of Hiroshima

1. Statement made by Betty Jean Lifton, reply to correspondence (New York, N.Y., 19 February, 1976).

2. Ibid.

14. The Decision to Drop the Bomb

1. "It Better Be Good," *Newsweek*, 9 May 1955, pp. 84, 85.

2. "Mouse at Yucca Flat," *Newsweek*, 16 May 1955, p. 63.

3. Fred Freed and Len Giovannitti, *The Decision to Drop the Bomb* (New York: Coward McCann, Inc., 1965), p. 133.

4. Ibid., p. 312.

5. John Toland, *The Rising Sun* (New York: Random House, 1970), p. 765.

6. Freed and Giovannitti, p. 255.

7. Ibid., p. 282.

8. Robert Jay Lifton, *Death in Life: Survivors of Hiroshima* (New York: Random House, 1967), p. 333.

9. Toland, p. 766.

10. David G. Yellin, *Special* (New York: Macmillan Co., 1972), p. 145.

11. Ibid., p. 165.

12. Ibid., p. 147.

13. Ibid., p. 258.

14. Alan Rosenthal, *The New Documentary in Action* (Berkeley: University of California Press, 1971), p. 151.

15. Yellin, p. 37.

16. The War Game

1. Peter Watkins, *The War Game* (New York: Avon Books, 1967), p. 59.

2. Paul Gardner, "The Horror That Shook the British Isles," *New York Times*, 3 April 1966, sec. 2, p. 2.

3. Michael MacDonald, "After Armageddon," *New Republic*, 13 May 1967, p. 34.

4. John Hershey, *Hiroshima* (New York: The Modern Library, 1946), pp. 12, 13.

5. Watkins, p. 59.

6. "Children of the Bomb," *St. Louis Post Dispatch*, 8 August 1971, p. 10 (Parade Section).

7. Jeff Rosenberg, Jim Russell, and Connie Wetzel, "All Things Considered," A National Public Radio Program aired on 6 August 1971, WSIE-FM, Edwardsville, Ill.

8. Ibid.

9. Gardner, p. 2.

10. Winifred Crum Ewing, BBC producer of documentaries, personal interview, Edwardsville, Ill., 9 November 1971.

11. Patricia Marx's forty-five minute audio tape interview with Peter Watkins (date and station not known).

12. Ibid.

13. Ibid.

14. Ibid.

15. Rosenberg, Russell, and Wetzel.

16. Ibid.

17. Moria Walsh, "The War Game," *America*, 6 May 1967, p. 703.

18. Dwight MacDonald, "Politics," *Esquire*, November 1967, p. 211.

19. Walsh, p. 703.

20. Stephen Vincent Benét, *The Last Circle* (New York: Farrar and Straus, 1946), p. 107.

17. Footnotes on the Atomic Age

1. William Bluem, *Documentary in American Television* (New York: Hastings House, 1968), p. 89.

2. Ibid., p. 98.

3. Ibid., p. 104.

4. Ibid., p. 117.

5. Alexander Walker, *Stanley Kubrick Directs* (New York, Harcourt Brace Jovanovich, 1971), p. 188.

18. "Net Journal": *Hiroshima-Nagasaki*

1. Paul Anderson, *Thermonuclear Warfare* (Derby, Conn.: Monarch Books, Inc., 1963), p. 32.

20. Hiroshima-Nagasaki—August, 1945

1. Erik Barnouw, "How A University's Film Branch Released Long-Secret A-Bomb Pic," *Variety*, 5 January 1972, p. 24.
2. Richard M. Barsam, *Nonfiction Film* (New York: E. P. Dutton, 1973), p. 203.
3. Barnouw, p. 24.
4. Ibid.
5. Statement made by Dale Wile, National Educational Television: reply to correspondence (Ann Arbor, Mich., 19 December 1972).

21. To Die, To Live

1. Phone interview with Dr. Robert Jay Lifton, 25 October 1976.
2. Ibid.
3. John Leonard, "Looking Back at Hiroshima Makes Uneasy Viewing," *New York Times*, 1 August 1976, sec. D., p. 1.
4. Lifton invitation to American premiere screening, Museum of Modern Art, 4 May 1976.

23. Arms and Security: How Much Is Enough?

1. Ramsdell Gurney, Jr., "Negotiating for Peace," *Commonweal*, 15 December 1972, p. 246.
2. *Only the Strong*, a 1972 television documentary produced by the Institute for American Strategy, Boston, Va.
3. *New York Times*, 4 August 1972, p. 1.

24. Only the Strong

1. *Broadcasting*, 5 November 1973, p. 3.
2. "Free T.V. Time Aids Drive by Foes of Arms Control," *New York Times*, 16 November 1972, p. 16.
3. "T.V. Arms Promotion," *St. Louis Post Dispatch* (editorial), 22 November 1972, p. 18B.
4. Ibid.
5. "Arms and Security: How Much Is Enough?" transcript of ABC documentary, p. 56.
6. *New York Times*, p. 16.
7. Films expressing other points of view may be found at the Hiroshima/Nagasaki Memorial Collection at Wilmington College's Peace Center in Wilmington, Ohio, notably ABC's 1965 documentary, *Hiroshima—20 Years After*.

Index